The Power of Dignity

Stories of Courage and Hope
Combating Child Trafficking in Nepal

SILVIO SILVA
With Sarah Symons

The Power of Dignity: Stories of Courage and Hope Combating Child Trafficking in Nepal
Copyright © 2024 by Silvio Silva and Sarah Symons
All rights reserved.

No part of this publication may be reproduced, stored in a retrieval system, or transmitted, in any form or by any means, electronic, mechanical, photocopying, recording or otherwise, without the prior written permission of the author, except in the case of brief quotations embodied in critical articles and reviews.

Some names used in this book have been changed to respect the privacy of the individuals.

Independently Published in 2024 by Silvio Silva and Sarah Symons

Edited by Arielle Ratzlaff
Cover Design and Typesetting by Arielle Ratzlaff
Cover Photo and Author Portrait by Eric Davis

ISBN: 9798327144002

The Power of Dignity

Silvio Silva with Sarah Symons

Arise, cry out in the night, as the watches of the night begin; pour out your heart like water in the presence of the Lord. Lift up your hands to him for the lives of your children, who faint from hunger at every street corner.

(Lamentations 2:19, NIV)

Dedication

To the Lord, who gave me an abundant life and hope. To my dear wife, Rose, the apple of God's eyes for my life, who always dares to dream with me and face all the challenges, whether with many resources or few. To Davi Asafe, my dear son, who brings me joy with his pastoring and friendship. To my daughter, Asha, who brought more love, color, music, dreams, hope and joy into our lives. For Asish, who added dreams to our lives.

To Dr. José Rodrigues, who had this dream first and shared it with us and many others.

To our beautiful team that works with me in Nepal and, of course, the girls and boys that we serve. Without them, nothing would be possible. Those who were helped at the beginning now return love to us, multiplying our efforts through their own vision and hard work. They teach us every day about love and hope.

To the volunteers who help us to lay every brick to this "building", and to the friends who share their bread, who finance these ambitious and expensive dreams for the children of Nepal.

To the people of Nepal, the many friends and family that we have there. Even in difficult times with some who were against us, we learned to love and respect them. We are especially thankful for the Nepalese people who are our family. Many celebrated with us, many wept with us, many fought with us. We thank you all.

Contents

Foreword	1
May, 2011	9

PART 1

1 How I Got Here	15
2 Lost in Translation	21
3 The First Generation	31
4 Our Family Grows	41
5 Stories of Hope and Transformation	55
6 Learning to Dream	67
7 The Dream Crosses New Borders	77
8 Asha	87
9 Embracing Change	101

PART 2

10 Understanding the Why and the How	115
11 Homecoming	131
12 The Earthquake	145
13 The Dream Continues	159
Epilogue	173
Your Invitation	183

Foreword
by Randy Watson

I had no idea that meeting Silvio nine years ago would be the greatest source of change and continuous growth in my life. He has helped me understand the deep longings I've carried to help others, and he has spoken clarity into the confusion I've struggled with around the suffering of humanity. I'm profoundly grateful for the influence that his life and leadership has had on me.

Ending human trafficking isn't about brute force, raids or many of the things you've heard from Hollywood movies. Ending human trafficking starts with changing how we see people. It's about de-commoditizing each other. This is what Silvio and his family have spent their lives doing—and they've changed the course of thousands of people's futures because of it. If you picked up this book because you care about ending human trafficking, I hope you finish it with a deeper conviction to sacrifice for others, to get closer to things that make you uncomfortable and to give of yourself without the thought of receiving anything in return.

Outside of business, I had spent a decade volunteering and supporting various charities both in the West and in the Global

South. I had seen beautiful and horrifying things while serving on the ground in conflict zones, in situations of extreme poverty and after devastating natural disasters. And I had met some truly remarkable people who were leading in all of these contexts.

But Silvio and his team were different. When I first met him in 2015, I was immediately captivated by his humor, kindness and ability to see and meet the needs around him. He and his wife Rose had already been working in the anti-trafficking space for 15 years, with a focus on providing long-term safe housing and restoration for children.

When it comes to anti-trafficking efforts, providing long-term care for survivors is often overlooked because of the huge commitment it requires. In Silvio's words, "Many times the reality contradicted the romantic notions that we once had about this type of work. It was hard to work with extremely damaged children in a culture and context so different from our own. We had to teach them the most basic life skills, even how to turn off a faucet so it wouldn't keep running."

When I asked Silvio how he would define his role and purpose, he said, "I'm just trying to be a loving father to these children." I've witnessed him live out that purpose over the past decade in the way he postures himself. While doing some of the most difficult work you could imagine, he's remained tender, confident and somehow kept his childlike humor.

As a native Portuguese speaker, Silvio had to learn to speak English and understand Nepalese in order to work in the country and communicate the needs internationally. You'll learn in this book that language learning did not come easily for him. Despite this, he is able to communicate with deep empathy and timely humor across languages.

FOREWORD

In our first weeks together, I noticed he would often finish a story or statement by saying, "Understand?" I could tell he had a deep desire to speak clearly and make sure his feelings and knowledge were being interpreted correctly. Communicating across languages and cultures requires real commitment and humility. You have to accept that you'll be misunderstood and, at times, may even offend the person you're trying to help. You have to risk being wrong, own it when you are, and be first to put in effort toward the next step forward.

Silvio has helped me understand what it means to be human—the physical, mental and spiritual aspects that make us come alive, give us purpose and enable us to love and sacrifice for others. He has demonstrated this not just with words, but through real, vulnerable action as he works to prevent one of the most devastating injustices of our day: child sex trafficking.

It's easy to take the opportunities and privileges surrounding us for granted if we aren't paying attention. I distinctly remember a conversation Silvio and I had a few years ago about the events of the 2015 Nepal earthquake. We were discussing how exhausted Silvio and his team had been in the immediate aftermath. Their own homes had been relatively unaffected, so they had deployed all the staff to help those in need. Silvio told me that after the first few sleepless weeks of helping he noticed he was becoming easily irritated. He decided to stop what he was doing and drive to an area with some of the most devastation. "I needed to get closer to the suffering," he explained. "I had to be reminded of what my perspective needs to be." His sensitivity to notice indifference creeping in and his quickness to address it are why he's been able to stay present and grounded in this work for decades.

This idea has become a guiding principle in my own life:

Being proximate to both suffering and to those who are different from you keeps you human. It builds empathy, removes prejudice and keeps you focused on things that matter. "Getting closer to the suffering" keeps you aware of both the opportunities and the privileges that are ever-present.

A year after Silvio and I met, his organization in Nepal faced severe financial difficulties. The situation was so dire that it led me to leave my construction business and establish a charity called Ally Global Foundation to ensure the work in Nepal could continue, expand and become more self-sustaining. Ally has now grown to support anti-trafficking work in Cambodia and Canada (where we're based) as well, but we exist because of the influence of Silvio and his family.

I never imagined my life would become so intertwined with the family of people you'll hear about in these pages. I hope this book leaves you with a deeper understanding of purpose, sacrifice and the ability each of us has to serve those around us. The experiences Silvio has taken the time to share here are the meaningful, real life stories of people he (and I) love dearly. They can feel heavy, even for those of us who live in this work every day. But I invite you to lean in all the same, and allow these learnings, musings and stories from my dear friend and mentor bring you closer to the needs around you and around the world.

Randy and Silvio in Nepal after the earthquake; 2016.

All names are changed in this book when sensitive or private stories are shared, and all stories are shared with permission.

May, 2011

As I waited all afternoon at a police station in Kathmandu, Nepal, I wondered, "How did I get here?" This was not the first time I had thought this, and it was far from the first time I had been in this situation.

I was there to fight for a young girl's life, for her right to walk free on this earth. Anaya had been trafficked from Nepal to Kolkata, India in her early teens. After several years of extreme, dehumanizing abuse, she was rescued in a raid. Eighteen months later, she was brought home to Nepal and placed in the care of our organization, The Apple of God's Eyes. I call it an "organization" and technically it is, but it's also a family—a big, loving, happy family with hundreds of kids who have been rescued from the streets, from human trafficking and from abusive situations of all kinds.

Anaya had been doing well with us. Then her mother appeared suddenly one day, accompanied by a man pretending to be a lawyer. She claimed that we had taken Anaya into our custody illegally. They wanted to take her back to Kolkata, where her mother owned a brothel, so that they could continue to use her and profit from her body. We would not let that happen. We fought hard against them, both at the police station and in the court.

Some of the people fighting the hardest alongside me to protect Anaya were young Nepali women who had grown up in our organization—former street children who have now taken on this mission as their own. I call it an "organization", and technically it is, but it's also a family—a big, loving, happy family with hundreds of kids who have been rescued from the streets, from human trafficking and from abusive situations of all kinds. I never imagined this would be my life.

PART I

Chapter 1
How I Got Here

For as long as I can remember, I have been fascinated by faraway lands and the diverse nations of the earth. I wasn't a good student in subjects like math or science, but I always loved history and geography. By age nine, I had memorized the capital of every country in the world.

My father put me to work at a very young age. He represented several newspapers in our small town of Ipora, Brazil, so at eight years old he had me delivering the paper. What started as just one street soon became over half the city. I hated delivering newspapers, because it meant I had to work after school when, like most Brazilian boys, I would have much rather been playing soccer.

Even when it rained heavily, the work had to be done. Sometimes I worked hard, selling extra newspapers in order to buy sweets or pastries. Other times, I threw all the newspapers in the sewer and went to play soccer! When subscribers complained that their newspaper never reached their home, I would make up some elaborate excuse.

Only one thing could soothe the pain of having to work at such a young age, and that was the fantasy I created that each street was a different country. When I was in a neighborhood where Japanese families lived, I would tell myself, "I'm in Japan." Where German families lived, I would pretend to be in Germany. Even though I loved Brazil (and would support them in every World Cup no matter what), I grew up with the dream of traveling to other nations.

In my teens and early twenties, my desire for adventure took me all over the country, from Sao Paulo to the Amazon jungle. In each city I would try a new job or start a new small business, but each one ultimately failed—some losses more devastating than others.

After a lot of troubles and mishaps, I found myself attending a church, where I had a powerful faith experience. Through this church I found a new purpose for my life, and I also found my beloved Rose, who became my wife in 1991. Things were going well. My business was quite successful at that time and it felt good to finally have some money flowing. But I felt pulled in another direction: I wanted to study to become a pastor.

After I left bible college, Rose and I were appointed to pastor a small town church in the state of Mato Grosso. We served there for four years, then moved to the capital city of Belo Horizonte in the state of Minas Gerais to work in another church.

We loved the work and the people, but our hearts were always moved toward the "nations of the earth." We also believed that our work as pastors went well beyond preaching and praying. We saw it as our responsibility, and our joy, to take people in and care for them in our own home. In particular, we felt called to care for children.

During our time in Mato Grosso State we learned about David, a little boy living in a children's home operated by some friends of ours. We met David when he was just four months old. It was love at first sight when he looked up at us with his toothless baby smile, and after another four months we became his legal guardians (the full adoption process would take another four years).

The following year, while David was still a toddler, we opened up our home even further. There were three girls coming to our church whose father had abandoned them, and their mother was an alcoholic. One day, one of the girls called us: "I have no place to go. My grandmother left me on the street."

Rose and I got in the car immediately to go help her. We were expecting to pick up just one child, but when we got there, the girl was waiting with her two sisters. Our apartment was small, but we couldn't turn them away. David came and slept on the floor of our room so that the three girls could move into his bedroom. We provided foster care for those three girls, and several others, for four years.

Around this time, a man named José Rodrigues came to speak at our church. Dr. José was both a pastor and a cardiologist. He used the profits from the two hospitals he owned to do international service work. In his sermon, Dr. José shared a shocking story from his recent trip to India.

He had been visiting the Kamitipura red light area of Mumbai, where he had been invited to set up a health clinic. One day, while walking through the area, he came across the body of a young girl lying on the sidewalk, naked and wrapped in a thin sheet. She appeared to be about twelve years old. Dr. José watched, horrified, as a man walked by pulling a garbage cart, picked up the girl's body and tossed it onto his pile of trash.

While Dr. José was beside himself, other bystanders just

shrugged and turned away. They didn't understand his distress. "She's just a Nepali whore," they said. Asking around about that girl, he learned she had been enslaved in forced prostitution. He also learned that there were thousands of other girls living in subhuman conditions on that same street—many of whom were trafficked from the neighboring country of Nepal. At that moment, Dr. José decided he would do whatever he could to help these girls find freedom from their enslavement and return to their home country.

When he got back to Brazil, he told anyone who would listen about the girl on the Mumbai sidewalk. He cried as he shared the story with our church. I was moved, of course, but I didn't think it had anything to do with me. I couldn't see what business we had with girls in Nepal when there were so many kids on the street in Brazil who also needed help.

A few years later, Dr. José visited our church again and, once more, told the story about the girl in Mumbai. "Please, we have to do something," he urged us as he talked about all the Nepali girls trapped in the red light areas of India.

Hearing the story for a second time, I started to feel some internal pressure to take action—but I certainly wasn't ready to drop everything and move to Nepal. So it was a relief when another couple from our church volunteered to go, and I felt I could contribute by providing some financial support. Even so, we thought about human trafficking in Nepal a lot over the next few years.

By this time, Rose and I had built a comfortable life for ourselves. We had a nice car and had moved into a bigger apartment. Our life was good, but we had begun to feel less fulfilled in the work we were doing in Belo Horizonte. I had become frustrated as a pastor because people were so obsessed with soccer that we had to schedule everything around the timing of the games. I love this sport too, but it felt out of balance.

I had recently visited and spoken in Mozambique, and people in the churches there seemed to have such open hearts and minds, and a true hunger for learning. So as Rose and I contemplated what it could look like to work "among the nations," Africa seemed like a natural place to start.

When Dr. José learned of our plans, he told us: "Please don't go to Africa. Go to Nepal. That couple from your church, they never actually went. The girls of Nepal need you."

Now, with the terrible suffering of these girls pressed on us for a third time, we felt compelled to change our plans. Instead of going to Africa, we would move to Nepal and work against child sex trafficking. With Dr. José supporting us through his non-profit, Missão Cristã Mundial (MCM), we would set up a home to support girls once they returned from the red light areas of India. We would provide a place for them to heal and assist them as they reintegrated into society.

And so, in November 2000, just forty-five days after making this decision, we got on a plane to Kathmandu, Nepal with all our worldly belongings in a few suitcases and $9,000 in our pockets—the result of selling our car and some generous donations. (One group of family friends raised money by selling the jewelry off their bodies!)

David was six years old when we arrived in Nepal. We spoke zero Nepali and only a few words of English. We had hardly ever traveled outside of Brazil, and we had little knowledge of the geography of Nepal or its culture. We were totally unprepared.

*Silvio, Rose and David arrive in Nepal
with Dr. José; November, 2000.*

Chapter 2
Lost in Translation

Those first 45 days in Nepal, living in a budget hotel with a six-year-old, were some of the hardest days of our lives. We had little money, no one to advise us and no idea where to begin the work of caring for trafficked girls. There weren't many modern comforts in Kathmandu at that time and gathering any items we needed was a struggle.

The hotel where we lived at first cost just $10 USD per day. It was all we could afford, and surely we got what we paid for. Next door, a nightclub would blast loud music every night into the early morning. We had to clean our room thoroughly to keep David from having severe asthma attacks.

One day, David became extremely sick and we were beside ourselves with worry. In the rush of leaving Brazil we had lost his asthma medicine. I didn't know what store to go to, or if the medicine would even be available in Nepal, but I went out at night to look. By some miracle, the asthma medicine he needed had the same name in Nepal as it did in Brazil (this was rarely the case). The medicine saved David's life that night. When everything else was extremely challenging, this small miracle gave us the courage we needed to carry on.

When people decide to go work in a foreign country, they usually put in some effort to prepare themselves. They may even spend several years learning the language and studying the culture, geography, people and challenges of the place where they are going. Because our approach had been much more spontaneous, we tried to approach everything with an open mind and a humble attitude. We didn't arrive in Nepal thinking we had all the answers, and I believe, in our case, that was a good thing, because it allowed us to learn as we went along.

In the days before we left Brazil, Rose had been very nervous. She worried that she wouldn't know how to take care of trafficked girls. She did not understand their culture and she could not begin to understand what they had endured. But she was determined to give her all. Dr. José had reassured Rose that she didn't need to be a professional social worker or international development expert. What the girls would need most was a mother.

To get started, we hired a translator and connected with some social service agencies, asking them to refer girls to us who were survivors of trafficking. Soon, one of the agencies sent two girls. We took them into our home and got them into a good school. Communication was challenging at first, since we had limited Nepali and the girls had limited English, but Rose and I cared for them as a mother and father. One of the girls suggested we call the project "The Apple of God's Eyes." The phrase "apple of the eye" comes from the Bible. In Hebrew, the translation refers to the reflection of yourself that you can see in another person's eye. It has come to mean "cherished above all else." The girls who came to us had such low self-esteem. They felt worthless and had been abandoned and severely neglected or abused. We chose the name to show girls—from the minute they walked through our doors—that here they were cherished.

After a year and a half we had six girls living with us. We had to rely on our translator to understand their cases, and were told that each one was a survivor of sex trafficking. One girl, he said, had been trafficked into a Maoist guerrilla camp where she was abused by all the soldiers. The stories of the other five were equally horrific.

Each month, we sent reports home to Brazil, to Dr. José and the other people supporting the work, so they could learn about the impact of their donations.

Meanwhile, we were becoming suspicious that our translator was not translating accurately. He had told us our visa process was in progress, but when we went to the consulate we learned that no papers had been filed on our behalf. The Nepali people who joined our team also began telling us that the translator was not good, so we decided to hire a new one.

When we had the new translator ask the girls some questions about their experience of trafficking, they looked utterly confused. "What are you talking about?" they said.

And so we discovered, to our shock and horror, that the first translator and the people who referred the girls to us had made all the stories up! They had been taking advantage of the fact that we didn't speak Nepali and were just learning the culture. In fact, not one of the six girls living in our home had ever been trafficked. They came from poor families, and they had come to live with us because they were promised they could get a good education. One of them had been a victim of sexual abuse, but not trafficked. Of course, we were happy they had not gone through the horrific experience of sex trafficking, but we were devastated that we had unknowingly been lying to our supporters in Brazil.

I felt that I should confess this to MCM (Dr. José's organization in Brazil that had been supporting us) immediately, so I called them and explained the hard truth we had just learned. Dr José understood, but he alone could not keep the plans afloat, and some others were not as understanding. In their eyes, the project was a failure. The goal had been to provide care specifically to survivors of trafficking. We had now been in Nepal for two years, and had failed to do this. They told us to close the doors of the home and return to Brazil immediately. It was a terrible time. Our reputation was damaged and our integrity was being questioned. Everything we had worked so hard to build seemed to be falling apart. We felt extremely sad and defeated.

They told us to give up the lease on our house in Kathmandu, as most of our sponsors were no longer interested in financing the project. But we weren't ready to give up yet. We did not end our lease, and we agreed to return to Brazil on one condition: they had to buy us return plane tickets. In the cases where it was possible we reintegrated the girls we had been caring for to their families, but three of them had nowhere to go. We let the three girls stay in our house and hired a local woman to look after them while we traveled back to Brazil. We felt awful leaving the girls behind. They had become like family to us. As we left for the airport, the girls were sobbing, saying, "You are our father and mother. Please, please don't go."

While we were back in Brazil, a pastor friend gave us an unexpected gift. Some people had recorded a music album to raise money for anti-trafficking efforts, and now, despite others viewing our work as a failure, these people wanted to share the funds they had raised with us. It was $2,400. "Take the money and try again to do something in Nepal," Dr. José advised me.

Returning to Nepal with almost no money and no support was not a promising situation. But at least we had the plane tickets and $2,400 in cash. That would be enough money for the seven of us (myself, Rose, David, the three girls, and our Nepali caretaker) to survive for two months. And miraculously, in those two months, things began to turn around. We cut all ties with the agency that had tricked us, moved into a bigger house and began again. Though we didn't have much money, a kind man named Binod rented a house to us in a good neighborhood of Kathmandu called Hattigauda. He decided to trust us when no one would, which made it possible for us to start over.

We learned about a gang in Kathmandu that was forcing street children to beg. Every evening, the gang members would come and take all the money the kids had collected. Rose took on that gang. One by one, she began rescuing girls and bringing them into the care of our home. Soon we had 16 girls living with us.

It was exciting and deeply satisfying to see our work growing, to see the girls healing and truly thriving. But the finances were always my biggest stress. When Christmas came that year, we couldn't afford to buy presents for all the kids. Thankfully, we got a good deal on some nice, warm socks and mittens from the market. The girls were so happy to be given even these simple gifts. I will never forget their joy—it was the ultimate lesson in gratitude. It may sound silly, but that truly was our reality in those early days.

God always provided for our needs, but our needs just kept growing. I would raise money to care for nine girls, but by the time the money arrived, we would have 16. Then I would fundraise for 16 girls, but soon we would have 26.

Before the days of ATM machines, I would have to see the clerk at the bank to take out cash. Each week I would go in, ask for $500 or $600, and wait nervously as the lady would swipe my credit card. Usually, the machine would decline the transaction due to insufficient funds. The clerk was so kind about it. "Can I try a smaller amount?" she would delicately say. She would then allow me to cross out the original amount on the slip and try smaller and smaller amounts until it finally worked.

At one especially low point, I had to borrow money from one of our Nepali staff in order to pay the rent. I felt ashamed that we weren't able to sustain the project. Once again, Rose and I discussed the possibility of closing the home and returning to Brazil, but we hated the idea of giving up. Month by month there were more girls relying on us, some of them with extreme trauma. What's more, we had been doing the work long enough now to see the true transformative power of our love and care in their lives. So we prayed for a miracle that would enable us to keep going.

For the first three years we lived in Nepal, anytime I saw a story related to trafficking in the newspaper I would save it. I decided to use those stories to write a book and publish it in Brazil. I did not want to retraumatize our girls by asking them to tell their own stories, so I used the pieces I had collected from the news—stories that had already been publicly shared—and added insight from my own experience. I wrote that book in just one week.

It turned out to be quite successful, raising thousands of dollars, which got us through the funding crisis. The book also found its way into the hands of a precious new friend, Joliam, who pastored a Brazilian church in Pennsylvania. His congregation soon became loyal donors. Their generosity was inspiring because many members of Joliam's congregation were recent immigrants to America. They didn't make a lot of money, but what they did have they gladly shared with us and our girls.

The first thing we did with those donations was put all our girls in private school. Up until that point they had been in government schools, which were free, but often unwelcoming and disrespectful toward our children. Teachers would talk about our girls' backgrounds in front of the whole class. Sometimes the schools would refuse to admit them, saying they would be a bad influence on other students. Sometimes male teachers would make lewd comments which were deeply humiliating. All of this poor treatment made the girls afraid to go to class. It was a huge improvement in their lives when we were able to send them to private school.

Rose was determined to learn Nepali. She hated depending on others, especially after being tricked by that first translator. Though the Nepali language was difficult, Rose devoted herself to picking it up as quickly as possible. At first, she couldn't find any teacher to help her because her only language was Portuguese (at that time we spoke almost no English). She studied on her own, learning whatever she could from anyone who would help her, whether it was the waiter at the restaurant or the lady at the grocery market. Eventually, she was able to find a proper teacher. Rose's ability to learn the language was truly remarkable to me. It is, sadly, not a gift that I share. I was able to learn English, but never got good at Nepali.

Another challenge was maintaining visas to live in Nepal. In those first years we had student visas, which required continuous study at a local college. I had never played any instrument in my life, and I can now say with absolute certainty that music (like languages), is not my gift. Rose was supposed to be the one studying, as she had some training in piano, but the guy at the consulate wrote my name down instead of Rose's as the student, and then refused to change it. So for three never-ending years, I had to study classical guitar!

It was a two-hour trip to the college, and I had to go there for class twice a week. Truly, I had no ability. After studying the guitar for three years, I still could not play a single song. The day I finally played "Love me Tender" my teacher actually cried. "If I can teach music to you, I can teach anyone," he said through his tears.

Even with my guitar skills finally emerging, I was never sure if I would get my next visa. Every six months we had to go back to immigration for a renewal. The girls would wait at home, hoping we would succeed so we could stay with them and continue to be their parents. When I got home they would ask, "Good day or bad day?" The situation was so precarious and scary because the more time passed, the harder it was to contemplate going back to Brazil and leaving these precious girls behind.

As the program grew, Rose never wavered from her vision that a loving family environment, not a shelter, was what our girls needed most. "My calling in Nepal is to be a mother, not a social worker," she always said. "A mother is not someone who works so many hours and then goes home. It's a 24 hour job. You give yourself completely."

In many cases, anti-trafficking work was very institutionalized and aftercare programs were offered in a very structured and bureaucratic way. They lacked the touch of compassion. We found that, more than just shelter, food and legal aid, rescued girls needed love, attention and a kind word. They needed to have their stories heard. They needed to share their losses, their frustrations and, later, their growing dreams for the future.

Rose and I lived with the girls in a family setting. Yes, we had misunderstandings, financial problems and many other challenges, but we faced these as a family. Rose was with the girls 24 hours a day—teaching them, loving them, listening to them, correcting them when they misbehaved, watching TV, doing schoolwork with them—just like any other family. Her kitchen counter was her counseling office. She was always available if the girls needed her. In the loving environment of our home, we began witnessing girls heal from the trauma of their past and thrive.

Chapter 3
The First Generation

As our home grew, word spread among the vulnerable children and families of Kathmandu. Almost daily we received new requests to provide shelter. The majority of these cases came from people who did not understand the profile of the girls we aimed to serve. Parents wanted to place their children in our house because of the good opportunity for a comfortable home, food and quality education. Though it was difficult to turn people away, we knew we needed to stay committed to our goal of helping girls affected by trafficking.

At that time, the girls in our family were not trafficking survivors, but were at high risk of being trafficked. They were prevention cases—such as the girls rescued from the gang, girls who were the daughters of women in forced prostitution and girls who had lost one or both of their parents. These children were at real risk of falling into the hands of a trafficker.

When girls first came to live with us they were often melancholy and quiet. Sure that they would only be betrayed again, they were afraid to dream and wake up in a nightmare.

The profile of most girls who came to us was this: They

arrived with only the clothes on their backs. They didn't know how to use the shower or the toilet. They were desperately hungry and infested with lice. Simple things like taking a bath or wearing clean clothes were challenges to be conquered because they were so accustomed to life on the streets or growing up in red light areas where their mothers were exploited.

Many times the reality contradicted the romantic notions we once had about this type of work. It was tough caring for children with such deep trauma in a culture and context so different from our own. We had to teach them even the most basic life skills, like how to turn off a faucet.

Girls would arrive not knowing how to care for their belongings or themselves. They appeared disconnected and indifferent to every good thing they were given, as if it would end all too soon. We gave them nice clothes and school supplies, but they soon ripped or broke all the new things, as if they didn't believe they deserved them. They didn't want to stay clean. They refused to take a bath. I think unconsciously they thought, "I don't have the right to have this," or even, "This way of life is not for me. I am trash."

Assimilating new values—whether hygiene, friendship, self-worth or sharing responsibilities—was truly challenging for some girls, but we worked hard to help them overcome their self-destructive beliefs through teaching and modeling love and respect. It took a long time. As they learned, we were learning too.

The girls who had experienced sexual violence were uncomfortable showering because it required them to undress, which was triggering for them. The housemothers had to gently but continuously persuade the new girls to wash their bodies and develop healthy habits.

Girls arrived malnourished and without a habit of healthy and regular meals. Many times, when they first came to our home, they would eat way too much and become ill. As the days passed, they would gradually progress and learn good habits.

When they discovered they had rights, some girls went to the opposite extreme and became demanding and uncooperative. There was no emotional equilibrium in their souls. We came to understand what the lack of a childhood had done to them.

On one occasion we gave all of the girls gifts. We gave the younger ones toys, and to the teenagers we gave things like perfume or scarves. We observed that one young lady, Anila, upon receiving her gift, looked longingly at the little ones' toys. They had received miniature kitchens or dolls with clothes to change. After a while, Anila left her gift and started playing with the younger kid's toys. Seeing this, we understood that she longed for the childhood that had been robbed from her. Once we fully understood this, we began doing everything we could to help girls experience the joys of childhood, regardless of their actual age. This was vital for them to be able to move forward.

We called the first girls who lived with us in those early years our "First Generation". I'll now share a few of their stories with you. The individual stories told here—and throughout this book—are all shared with permission. Names have been changed to protect and respect the dignity of the individual.

Richa

Because Richa grew up on the streets, she was used to living surrounded by garbage. When she first came to live with us she would go weeks without taking a bath. When we would give her clean clothes, she only wanted to destroy them. She could not believe that her life had any value. Her self-esteem was so low that she did not even think she deserved to eat good food. On one occasion, we found her eating the cat's food, which was on a little plate on the ground. She had already eaten a full meal of human food, but could not bear to see food just sitting there, uneaten.

Sometimes, Richa would lie on the ground, completely withdrawn and unresponsive. She only began the process of rebuilding her self-esteem when we gave her a doll to play with. That same week she started to dance with the other children. Within a few more weeks, she began going to school and making incredible progress.

Saili

Saili, thin and beaten, knocked on our door asking for shelter. At that time we did not have any beds available, so we asked her to come back the next month. "Having no beds" was the explanation we gave, but the truth was we didn't have the money for any more kids.

Saili came back after a month, but we still had no capacity to take her. She came again a month later, and again I told her that I was sorry, but there were no beds available. That's when she told us that our porch was warmer, more comfortable and safer than the place she was currently sleeping: on the sidewalk along a street. There was no sense in asking her to come back later. Her words, and her raw need, cut to my heart. We decided that, even though we couldn't afford it, we would give her and her friends a place in the house.

For several weeks Saili and her friends slept on the floor.

This went against our principle of giving a warm bed to each girl in our care. We believed that having one's own bed was an important part of restoring dignity. Thankfully, after some weeks, we managed to buy more beds.

During her first few days in our house, Saili picked up a guitar and started to pick out some notes. In no time she was playing simple songs and accompanying the other girls. I wanted to encourage her talent, so I hired a teacher to give her lessons on Saturdays. She began perfecting her skills rapidly. What I had studied for three long years and not succeeded in, Saili could do with grace and ease in just a few months. She began to compose her own music. Suddenly, she was playing and singing in Portuguese, Nepali and English. It was hard to imagine how this girl with such beautiful musical talent had been living on a sidewalk and washing dishes in a filthy restaurant.

Saili told us about the humiliation and fear she suffered when she used to live with her parents, who were both alcoholics. Because they were never able to pay rent, they frequently got evicted from their homes. Breaking down in tears, she told us about a night when the landlord had thrown all her family's possessions out on the streets, evicting them from his house because the rent was overdue. The dejected family had to walk through the city carrying all their pots and other possessions, as others watched them with scorn. "I never again want to walk with my pots," said Saili.

One night, Rose and I were driving with Saili through Thamel, the tourist district where Saili had once lived on the street. She showed us the exact place on the sidewalk where she used to sleep when her family had no home. Listening to her story, I became so distressed that I hit another car (thankfully no one was injured). I was astounded and distressed that such a precious diamond like Saili had been lost among such suffering. I felt happy that she was found and restored to wellness, but at the same time I worried that I was missing other diamonds.

Menuka

Menuka arrived to us bald and bedraggled along with her friend, Pritty. The girls had been sleeping on the grass outside the temple in Pashupatinath, the most famous of the Hindu temples in Kathmandu. At that time, the area around the temple was also famous for the sexual exploitation of children. Rose spent a lot of time talking to the girls, and eventually convinced them to leave behind their life of thieving and selling their bodies for food.

On their first day with us, they got sick because they ate too much. They were not used to having consistent meals. On the streets, there had been many days where they only had enough money for a cup of tea. After a few months with us, Pritty returned to the streets, but Menuka stayed.

Like most of the girls living with us, Menuka did not know when her birthday was, so we chose a random date and decided it would be her birthday. On that day, as she cut her first birthday cake, we saw a beautiful young lady, smiling and happy, who had dreamed of better days just like this one.

Rose had a lot of difficulty enrolling Menuka in school. The private schools would not accept her and the government schools were hesitant because she was thirteen years old and had never studied before. Finally, after some resistance, one school accepted her. She went directly into fourth grade, because the school principal thought it would be embarrassing for her to study with six and seven-year-olds.

Even though she was a quick-thinking girl, this big jump made school especially challenging for Menuka. It was a psychological battle too. When she couldn't move ahead, she would fall back to feelings of, "I am not capable. I will never be anything." Our biggest challenge with Menuka was showing her that she *was* able.

When the time came for final exams at school, the challenge seemed too much. Many times Menuka talked about quitting. In Nepal, students were often beaten by their teachers and parents when they were not successful in their exams. We told Menuka that she was not obligated to pass, and that she would not be punished if she failed. All we asked was that she give her best. We counseled her that this was her first year in school and that, if she had to repeat the grade, it wouldn't be so bad, since she had started in fourth grade. This was an important conversation to help her not feel pressured, and to feel seen and valued just as she was.

One day Menuka went out to buy milk. While she was out, another girl arrived home with the results of everyone's final exams. I waited for Menuka at the gate of our house. When she came back from her errand, I showed her the sealed report card. She trembled. She was sure she had failed. But when we opened the envelope, we saw that she had passed and moved up to the fifth grade! Everyone rejoiced and Menuka became emotional. She had managed to do what seemed impossible in her eyes.

After almost a year with us, Menuka's mother was located. She was shocked to see her daughter clean, well dressed and looking so beautiful. The last time she had seen Menuka the picture had been very different. Menuka's transformation brought her to tears.

The photos we have of Menuka when she first arrived at our home show a young girl bald from stress. Over time, she grew into a beautiful young lady with long hair and a life full of dreams.

Manisha

Manisha was about 16 when she showed up at our door, asking us to take in her little sister, age 14, who was addicted to drugs. After just a few days with us the sister ran away and began using drugs again. But Manisha brought her back. This happened again and again. Manisha begged her sister to stay, telling her how beloved she was, but the girl just couldn't seem to stabilize.

When I saw Manisha weeping in desperation because of her love for her little sister, I felt compelled to talk to her. "Hey, why don't you stay here too? Stay and look after your sister inside this house. God is looking out not just for your little sister—this opportunity is for you too!" Manisha cried even harder. She also needed to feel loved. She had felt so drained from taking care of her three younger sisters and little brother. Because their parents were alcoholics, Manisha had been caring for her siblings since she was very small.

So Manisha stayed with us too (and so did the rest of her siblings eventually). She would grow up to become one of our most committed leaders, always finding ways to help others, even strangers.

In caring for Richa, Menuka, Saili, Manisha and the other thirty girls from the early years, we learned what was required to help children heal from extreme trauma. We weren't perfect; we made many mistakes. We had little money and the challenges were constant. Yet, despite our struggles and lack of experience, there was much love and much respect in our home. We became a family. And for those First Generation girls, it was enough.

Some of the First Generation; 2004.

Our old van was always full; 2004.

Chapter 4
Our Family Grows

In 2001, we met a 16-year-old named Mamata Tamang when she and her parents attended the same church service as us. Mamata was bold and inquisitive—sometimes to the point of being a little impolite. But her English was much better than mine, so one year later, when we found ourselves in need of a new translator, Mamata took on the job. Her strong, insistent personality could be challenging at times, but she took her work very seriously.

Then, in 2003, the caretaker we had hired to help us in the home quit to get married. Mamata immediately came to talk to us. "I will come and live and work with you guys," she said, with complete confidence. "I want to do anti-trafficking work. I have to do this work and I want to work with you guys."

"Thank you, but no," I told her. "We don't need your help right now."

But this stubborn young woman would not take no for an answer. She squeezed herself into our home, saying she would only stay for a few weeks, to help cover us in the transition. We didn't hire Mamata. She hired herself!

One day I said, "Okay, I'm thinking of hiring you for real, but if you want to work for us you have to be willing to do anything. You even have to be ready to clean the septic tank, whatever it takes."

I was speaking figuratively. I didn't really expect her or any staff member to do that. Mamata replied, "I am ready, you can count on me."

A short time later, some heavy rains caused the septic tank to back up and overflow. To bring a truck to empty it would have cost 5,000 rupees ($50), and we didn't have that in our budget. So I got a small pump and every day, morning and night, I had to pump out the water and transfer it into the sewage system outside. The smell was horrible. Mamata started to help me, and after a few days she started doing it alone. She would wake up before me to pump it in the morning, and when I would go to do it in the evening, she would have already beat me to it. My joke about the septic tank became real.

Mamata worked faithfully without a salary for many months. Now, she has been a part of our staff family for 22 years, and we could not imagine this work without her! She is a bright light in the lives of many, many girls, and in my life too.

We used to think Mamata was great only at administrative things. She is indeed very organized and does everything in a professional way. But her greatest strength is that she is deeply committed. She stands for love.

One day, Mamata went out to get a passport for one of the girls while there were riots happening in the streets. People were getting beaten, even killed, but she wouldn't turn back. She refused to come home until she got that passport. Mamata is a person of the deepest integrity. She has always lived according to her values. She would lay down her life for the girls.

OUR FAMILY GROWS

In 2004, our friends Sheyla and Lucas came to visit from Brazil. At the same time, Rose had to go on a trip to America to visit our supporters. I thought it would be inappropriate for me to be alone at the house with the girls while Rose was away (we didn't always have another staff member living with us), so I convinced Lucas and Sheyla to stay with me one month longer.

By that point, our home was overflowing with more than 50 girls. We desperately needed a second home to give them more space—and to be able to take in more kids—but we didn't know who to trust to run it. We had been tricked and cheated once, and were still wary.

Soon I started to notice things like Sheyla combing the girls' hair or Lucas fixing our car and motorbike. This was the type of help we needed, people who would treat our girls as their own and jump right in to help. So I asked them to think about returning to Nepal for a longer time. "Why not come back, and be the houseparents for a second home?" I suggested.

Sheyla had a background in education at a high level, but was currently working as Dr. José's administrative assistant. She and Lucas had both been successful in their careers, taken early retirement and were now working at MCM purely for the joy of service. I tempted them with the fact that there was *even more* service to be done here in Nepal. Dr. José got quite annoyed with me for stealing his assistant, because Sheyla and Lucas went back to Brazil, packed their things and moved to Nepal.

As soon as Rose got back from America, we opened Home 2 with Lucas and Sheyla as houseparents. Before long, there were 30 kids in that home.

It was incredibly comforting for us to have these lovely

friends come, who could speak our own language and were experienced parents, having already raised their own kids. We had been struggling on our own for five years, with little adult companionship. We thought Sheyla might not like it in Nepal or would find it difficult to adjust, because she was very ladylike and sophisticated. But she and Lucas had lived on a farm, so they knew the other side of life. Both of them fit in easily. They were simple, generous people, patient and gentle with the kids. We had been very isolated, but with them beside us, understanding the situation, we could fight our battles better. They ended up staying in Nepal for nine years.

It was only a couple years before Home 2 also reached capacity, and we once again needed to expand. To our surprise, Mamata and Marcia (one of our First Generation girls) asked for the opportunity to be the leaders of the third Apple of God's Eyes home. They were just 22 and 18 years old. I had been thinking we needed to find a married couple to be the houseparents—that was the model we were used to. I had in fact been looking for a Nepali couple to run Home 3. But then Mamata and Marcia approached us and said, "Instead of a couple, why not give us a chance to lead the house?"

I worried that might not sound good to our supporters. Mamata and Marcia were quite young, and our concept was that a home needed both a mother and a father. But these young women were very motivated. "Give us a chance," they asked. I still wasn't sure.

Weeks passed, and no one else came forward. The Nepali couples I interviewed seemed too conservative and rigid, too authoritative. It wouldn't have been a good fit. Our kids were used to a lot of freedom and a relaxed family atmosphere. We never controlled how they did their hair or what clothes they wore. We cared about their character. Those other things did not seem important. The Nepali couples we interviewed were scandalized by this approach. They wanted to crack down on the kids and run the home more like a boarding school or shelter. They would suggest things like waking the kids up at 5 a.m. But that just wasn't us.

We decided we needed to give our own young women a chance. In fact, the more we thought about it, the more we realized how special it would be to have a home run by people who grew up in our organization, who were already part of our family. We set up the new home by moving over some kids from Home 1, some from Home 2, and adding some newly rescued kids. The building we chose to rent for Home 3 was near our house so that we could help out if needed, but it turned out that Mamata and Marcia's home was very well managed. They didn't need us to oversee them, and the Home 3 kids were very happy.

Soon we had 120 children in our care across the three homes. They ranged in age from three to eighteen, most had serious trauma and they all needed a lot of attention. Because we were a larger than normal family, we had to establish some rules of coexistence and rhythms.

Each older girl would take one younger girl under her wing, and was called "Didi" (big sister). It was so beautiful to see the older kids helping the younger ones get ready for school in the morning. Our girls loved to go to school with shining shoes. This was not important to us, but it mattered a lot to them. Each house would use a whole can of shoe polish every day! There were so many shoes to shine. We were moved by this, because we saw how valued and important the children felt through having shiny shoes. This was a small piece of their dignity being restored.

Rose loved caring for the kids in our home as a mother:

> I was a very present parent in their lives. We played outside, did exercise together. Every evening was so pleasant. They did my hair. It was meaningful to be together. The kids didn't fight much. We had a few angry girls but mostly that was the exception. Much more than their bad behavior was their good behavior. Sometimes I played games with them and gave them a little bar of chocolate when they won. If I, as a Brazilian, won a chocolate, I would eat it by myself, because I had won it. That would be my right, and there would be nothing wrong with me eating it, in my way of thinking. But when any of our kids won a chocolate bar, that bar got broken into so many tiny pieces as they shared it with everyone. That was the most amazing thing, because these kids had been so poor and so deprived and yet still they were so generous. That was such a teaching for me. Nepalis love to share. It was beautiful to see. Anything you gave them, they made sure everyone got a bit. They never could eat something all by themselves.

Of course there were moments of frustration woven amongst many moments of joy; moments of profound stress followed by moments of profound accomplishment. Sometimes we got things right the first time, other times we made mistakes. We had nights of dancing, music and jubilation, and nights of sadness, regret and tears. But, as the program grew and grew, it was hugely gratifying to care for the children of Nepal and nurture their gifts and dreams. We saw them make fantastic progress as they learned about unity, all they could overcome in life and how to be a blessing to others. They grew to understand that they—and every other person on this earth—has dignity and human rights.

We never set out to be a shelter home or an institution of any kind. It would have been so much easier to just be social workers, providing food, shelter, education, rules and basic care. But we could not and did not do that.

"When the girls did right, I was the first one to praise them, to celebrate them," says Rose. "And when they did wrong, I was there to teach them, to say, 'You can do better.' Running homes in a family style is a job that no one wants. It's easier to create institutions. Creating a family requires your whole heart, your whole soul."

"We were not perfect. We had lots of mistakes and failures, but we never gave up on our values or our vision. We would tell the kids, 'You need to be there for each other, you need to fight for each other.' And I loved it when I saw the kids fighting for each other, calling each other sister and brother, taking the pain from one another."

Our kitchen counter was the counseling center. Rose would be cooking and the girls would come home from school and pour out their hearts and their hurts. She had a soul connection with them that lasts until this day. "They gave me their fear and their pain, and I gave it up to God," says Rose. "And somehow it was enough."

Rose almost destroyed some schools in Kathmandu, fighting for our kids. It gave the girls a sense of worth and belonging to know that someone was willing to fight for them. As they grew up I saw their hearts strengthen, because somebody was there for them. It heals the soul of a human being to know they are loved.

We encouraged the girls to study and develop their character. Everyone had to take part in chores to care for the house—this is part of belonging to any family. Even the little ones had little responsibilities. For the older ones, we established schedules for cooking and washing the dishes and clothes. With these activities, we wanted to teach them a sense of responsibility—doing your share for the family and community—as well as basic cleanliness and taking care of your physical space. Above all, we wanted the girls and staff to embrace the mentality of living together as a family in a home, not an institution.

While we always tried to maintain order, we also valued flexibility. The girls' daily routine, beyond schoolwork, English classes and chores, included plenty of time for play. In Nepal, women are expected to get up early in the morning, even during a rigorous winter or when they have no work to do. If they do not rise early, they are seen as lazy. Nepali women are woken around 5 a.m., at times needlessly. We woke our girls around 7 a.m. on school days and even later on weekends and holidays. People thought our timetable was too relaxed and often urged us to put the girls under a stricter schedule. But we didn't let other people's opinions change our house routine.

Nepali food is extremely spicy and saltless, and uses a spice combination called masala. As Brazilians we had different food preferences, but we didn't let this stop us from eating together as a big family. Meals usually included a wide variety of Brazilian and Nepali foods, and American foods, too, if we had volunteers or visitors from the USA. The real parties happened on the days we made pizza, which the girls loved above all other food. In this, I confess, we corrupted their culture. When we wanted to give the girls an incentive to study harder, all we had to do was promise that we would make pizza!

As soon as the girls were old enough to understand, we kept them informed and involved in all our activities, goals and projects as an organization. This too, people sometimes criticized, saying the girls were not worthy or mature enough to participate in these topics. But I always said, "Why not?"

So, whenever we received large or small donations or had new opportunities, we shared this information with the girls. We explained where we planned to use the donations, why we would use them in that way, how much we had and what we needed. Everyone had a voice and the opportunity to be heard. They were free to disagree, and often they did. We always took the time to talk things through and come to an agreement.

We tried to develop a spirit of gratitude in our kids toward those who helped us. We explained how expensive it was to maintain the work. We told them that, in many cases, people had to make sacrifices in order to contribute. We did this not to make them feel guilty or obligated to the donors, but so that they would think of others, cultivate a spirit of gratitude and understand the value of things.

Many Nepalis think all foreigners are rich and should give to Nepal because it's considered a poor country. We didn't want to raise entitled kids who took things for granted. We always shared very openly how much we had in cash and in the bank, how much we still needed and who was helping. We talked openly about money and expounded on the problems, options and solutions. The girls participated and knew about everything that was relevant to the program. After all, they were the reason for the work, and we believed it was just and worthy for them to participate in all aspects of it.

Other homes for rescued girls had armed guards, fences and electric gates. The Apple of God's Eyes had nothing like that. We didn't have locks on the gates or doors, and we never will. Some of these girls had been locked up, locked out and held back their whole lives. At Apple they got to be free. They got the chance to be kids and to be cared for, whether at five years of age or 19. We had rules, of course, but always like a family, not an institution. We always said that we have only a fence of love, and if that is not enough, nothing will be enough.

Another milestone came when we formed a local organization called Nepalese Home, operated entirely by local Nepali leadership. Nepalese Home took over the responsibility for supervision and support of The Apple of God's Eyes project in Nepal. This partnership gave us a better legal standing with the Nepali government and affiliation with the Social Welfare Council.

Mamata became the first President of Nepalese Home, alongside a group of the First Generation leaders who had grown up in our home. Once beneficiaries, now they were making the decisions, and they were deeply conscious of their responsibilities.

It was not easy to establish Nepalese Home. The first obstacle was that the girls did not have citizenship, and the second was that they each needed a police report saying they had no criminal history. Even after succeeding with both of these things, some government departments delayed in processing the organization's registration. This was probably because of prejudice toward the girls due to their backgrounds. Some of them came from indigenous groups—such as the Tamang—or lower castes that were not well respected in Nepali society.[1]

Many of our girls had been living on the streets, some had experienced sexual exploitation and all came out of extreme poverty. There was no law that prevented marginalized people from establishing a social welfare organization. It just wasn't customary, and there was a lot of resistance from local government officials. There was also discrimination based on the fact that our leaders were women, because Nepal was (and still is) an extremely patriarchal society.

However, one other survivor-established organization had succeeded in their plea for registration and had been operating for years. This strengthened our case, and Nepalese Home eventually also got approved.

Once we finally overcame these obstacles, we still had one more challenge. People were distrustful when they saw a new organization, formed by these unknown women from the lowest classes of society, receiving funding from an international organization. They feared two things: that the Nepali organization, led by inexperienced women, would use the resources poorly, and that the international organization would take advantage of the Nepali partnership and dominate the organization. This would go against Nepal's principle of sovereignty; they did not want to be dominated by foreigners, even in small decisions.

---

[1] The caste system is a rigid way of dividing people into hereditary classes, which determines what jobs they can do, who they can marry, where they can live and all other aspects of life. Though it was legally abolished by the Government of Nepal in 1963, its lingering effects are still very much present in the culture today.

THE POWER OF DIGNITY

Despite the discrimination, resistance and distrust by local people, Mamata and our First Generation leaders persisted. They had developed their own passion for serving the most vulnerable. Having been dismissed and devalued their whole lives, they would not be pushed aside. They have stood strong in their conviction from that day to this, and it has been my ongoing mission to champion and protect their autonomy.

Marcia and Mamata leading Home 3; 2007.

A full house; 2005.

Pizza night; 2005.

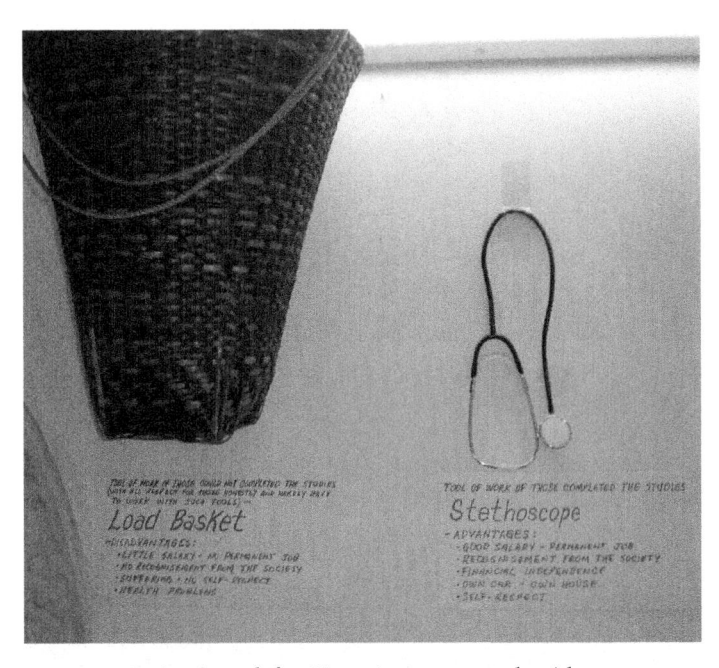

An iconic symbol at Home 1 to encourage the girls to study. I have nothing against the basket (doko), but it is such hard work and not a good income.

Chapter 5
Stories of Hope and Transformation

In the early 2000s and 2010s when we were starting the project, Nepal's culture was still very conservative. If a woman went walking on the street without a shawl over her shoulders people would be scandalized. Meanwhile, behind closed doors there was an epidemic of sexual abuse, often inflicted by a child's own parents and relatives. If a girl kept silent about the violence she suffered, she would avoid being blamed and shamed by society. But if she denounced her abuser, she would be seen as promiscuous and undeserving of help. Because of this, girls rarely spoke out about sexual abuse and children facing these situations had nowhere to turn.

This climate of silence and distrust greatly affected the girls who came to Apple. Having been used and betrayed from a young age, they lived under constant fear of being wronged again. Some girls arrived extremely wounded in their souls, distrustful and disbelieving that anyone in the world would ever help them. In the gentle, family environment of our homes, they were able to heal and become like children again. They learned to trust, to play and to be joyful. All of these transformations were incredible to witness, and some were truly miraculous.

Shanti

When Shanti came to live with us she was hostile and had a strong temperament. She soon won the nickname *Bicho-Brabo* (Angry Brat). A few months earlier we had received Shanti's older sister into our home. The older sister was six, and Shanti was just four years old. The girls had lost their mother in a kerosene stove explosion. At first, their father was very dedicated and kept the children with him. He worked as a stonemason and a pig farmer, and had no one to leave the children with when he went to work, so he would bring them along. The girls were always filthy with cement or slop from the pigs.

A woman in the community insisted several times that we take in the girls. Soon, the father himself pestered us to take them. One day, the father came to visit us. He had Shanti's older sister with him. I came to the door irritated, because I had already told him that we could not shelter his girls. I again explained, "We are not an orphanage. Our mission is to reach girls affected by trafficking." But the father insisted we shelter at least one of his children. Looking into that little girl's eyes, I sensed God saying to my heart, "Why don't you want to shelter her? She might not be your target, but she is mine." I immediately changed my tone and started the legal process to take her in. Everyone was surprised at my sudden change of opinion.

So Shanti's older sister joined our home. Two months later, we decided it would be cruel to take in just one sister and not both. So we took in Shanti as well. Time passed and each day we could see that Shanti and her sister were becoming more adapted and happy, attending school and eating well. We insisted that their father maintain a relationship with his daughters, so he would visit often.

Around this time I had been feeling quite down. Instead of running a large operation, as I had envisioned, I was taking care of plumbing and electricity, hanging clothes lines and picking up underwear and stockings that were thrown around the house. I felt like I was not seeing God's glory. I felt like I had moved here to do something bigger, but here I was doing mundane and annoying things that I wasn't even qualified for. I had imagined a project with a large, visible impact.

I reminded myself that when the glory of God was first manifested to Moses in a burning bush, it was a small thing, not a whole mountainside. But even with this in mind, I felt frustrated not seeing what I had wanted to see in my work. I even questioned if I should continue working in Nepal. I spent hours on the rooftop terrace brooding in these thoughts.

After fixing the clothesline at Home 1 for the third time that week, and feeling frustrated that even *that* wasn't being done right, I took a break to spend tea time with the girls. I had decided that I would make the girls tea every day that week, as a way to not to feel so useless. On this specific day I had picked up a special cream-filled pastry to go with the tea.

Shanti came home, and this pastry happened to be her favorite. Because of her difficult past—practically being raised in a pigsty—she had no manners and didn't know how to eat properly. She came inside, grabbed the pastry and started shoving it into her mouth. At the same time she started drinking tea, and there was food and liquid running all down her face and chest. The first thought that went through my head was, "Yuck, that is disgusting."

Then, I felt God say to me, "Remember the little burning bush? You wanted to see my glory...look again. *This* is my glory." This girl is safe, she is protected, fed and happy. I realized I had missed the point. There was glory all around me.

Watching this simple domestic scene of Shanti overflowing with bread and tea, feeling protected, fed and happy, I understood that this was the whole point. I was doing God's work and it was glorious. I went outside and had to hold myself up by the fence to cry in silence. In that instant, I understood something that changed my life. Regardless of how basic our accomplishments felt, regardless of the number of girls we were helping, I was fulfilling my mission. I understood that God's love often manifests in simple things or even in things that seem unimportant to human eyes. It can be seen and sensed in a drooling child who feels happy and protected.

Anna

Anna arrived in our midst with no toes on her left foot. She had lost them to an untreated infection when she was just a baby. The result—a deformed foot and limping walk—caused her to be scorned and excluded at school and on the streets. One day when Rose asked Anna to put on some sandals and go run an errand at the neighborhood store, Anna replied that she could not wear sandals because she did not have toes. We cried secretly upon hearing this.

Another time, Anna told us about a dream she had. In the dream she had been given a shiny, new foot. But how could this be possible? We had no money for that kind of operation. And besides that, it would have to be done in another country, because the Nepali medical system at that time did not have the capability to perform such a complicated operation.

One day, as I was preparing to leave for the USA, I noticed Anna playing with a doll made of old socks. I promised I would bring her back a real doll. During my trip, someone gave me a beautiful baby doll to give to Anna. When I arrived back in Nepal, Anna took that doll in her hands and wept for forty-five minutes straight. She had never had a real doll to play with, and now she finally had one. It was an unimaginable miracle to her.

I felt such overwhelming joy, seeing that child hugging her doll with so much passion, feeling loved because somebody remembered and cared about her dream of having a doll. But Anna still had a much bigger dream, a shiny new foot, and we did not yet see a way to give it to her. We hoped and prayed for a solution, but in the meantime we helped Anna adjust to her disability and work within the situation as it was.

Laila

Once in a while, Rose and I would go out for dinner to a nice restaurant in downtown Kathmandu. On this particular occasion, we decided to invite some of our girls, including Laila, to enjoy the evening with us. When we arrived at the restaurant everything proceeded as normal: the waiter brought the menu, left us to make our choices, then came back after several minutes to take our order. He was polite and treated everyone at our table with due respect, collecting orders from one person after another. Laila was one of the last to order. Until that moment, we didn't notice anything strange happening.

When the waiter left the table, Laila was covering her face with the menu and sobbing. We didn't understand what could be wrong. The moment was so special, the restaurant was great, yet she was crying convulsively. After taking a deep breath, she opened up to Rose. A couple of years earlier, before she lived with us, she used to go to this same restaurant to sleep on the porch behind the main door. She also used to search for food in their garbage bin when she was hungry, but a waiter would always throw her out and shout bad words at her. Here she was, years later, back at that same restaurant, but now sitting at a table as an honored guest. Instead of dirty clothes and uncombed hair, she wore clean clothes and had beautiful hair, and that same waiter didn't even recognize her as the girl he used to kick out.

It was a profound experience for Laila. It gave her a strong sense of her own dignity. Before, that restaurant and waiter had made her feel unworthy. Laila was in tears because, after being so humiliated, she was now feeling honored. She now had, quite literally, a seat at the table.

Eva

Eva, at 14 years old, sold purses in a tourist area in Kathmandu. She spoke enough English to approach potential clients. Being a working child in that area made her terribly vulnerable to trafficking and other forms of abuse. We hoped and prayed for many months that we would be able to bring her into the care of our home. I didn't know Eva personally at that point, but Rose and another team member always spoke about her as a sweet, outgoing girl who had captured their hearts.

One day, a girl who I didn't recognize approached me in our house, saying confidently, "Hello Uncle, how are you?" She used this familiar term as if she had known me a long time. I was quite confused, thinking, "Who is this girl?" Then Rose told me that this was Eva, the girl we had been hoping would come to live with us. She came and conquered all our hearts with her open and pure smile.

In September of 2006 I was in the hospital. After having kidney surgery, I had contracted an infection and was now suffering from a high fever, pain and deliriousness. While I was in this low state, I noticed that several of the girls were always right by my side: Laila, Kristina and Eva.

One particular day I was in a lot of pain and the doctors were worried. The infection was not going down even with a strong regimen of medication, and the pain was unbearable. Seeing me in that situation and fearing for my life, the girls started to cry. Rose recommended that they go to the house and ask the other girls to pray for me. My illness was truly life-threatening.

As I groaned from pain and fever, I sensed Eva coming close to the bed, along with Kristina, whispering, "Uncle, don't worry. You are not going to die. You are going to get better. You will be fine. You are going to go home. Do you know why? It's because we were so sad, and now we are happy. God told me I will never feel sad like that again. If you died, I would be sad. So I am quite certain that you will go home cured."

Despite all the pain, I cried with joy in that moment. How beautiful to hear those words. If I hadn't been in that hospital bed, I would not have heard those words and would not have known how much I was loved by the children. The next morning, the infection began to recede. Soon, the fever left me, and a few days later I went home cured.

Bella

When Bella first came to live at our home everything seemed to be going well for her. But after a few months, a man came to our gate saying he was her owner. He proceeded to threaten us for several months, spreading rumors around the neighborhood that our house was a brothel. He claimed to be friends with the authorities and even the king of Nepal. The case crept along, without a solution, for three long months. He delayed handing over Bella's identity documents and demanded damages of $1,300 for her. Unfortunately, bribery and extortion are extremely prevalent in Nepal. He insisted we pay this price in order to free her.

Once we realized that these threats weren't going to stop, we decided to present the case to the police. This put us in a precarious position, with a real risk of being expelled from the country. At that time, we were in Nepal on student visas. We were not citizens, and we had been having some challenges with our visas.

Besides this, our team was divided about how to handle the situation. Some thought the best option was to give Bella back to her trafficker, with the goal of freeing us from bigger problems. But how could we in good conscience do such a thing? Our entire purpose was to defend girls like this.

So we took the case to the police. Thankfully, after they came to understand the truth, we won the case. The man was quickly detained and required to return Bella's documents. It was an incredible joy when we succeeded in freeing Bella from the clutches of that man. The police actually compelled him to kneel at her feet and apologize! There was even a photo taken of him in that position. The gesture signified that he was returning to her the dignity he had stolen, and that she was innocent.

As girls began to heal in our care, a big challenge for Rose and I was helping them learn how to dream. The caste system in

Nepal was so strong, and the influence of that culture on them was so powerful. One of the biggest differences between Nepali culture and our own is this: in Western culture, if you make a mistake, you can put it behind you, whereas in Nepali culture, if you make a mistake, you are a bad person and will carry the shame forever. If you are born into a low caste, you can never rise above that. You are not supposed to dream for anything else. The kids had internalized these beliefs. They didn't expect to achieve above what their caste prescribed. It was so hard to help them understand that even if they had made mistakes, been in a red light area or come from a bad family, they still deserved to be happy and loved.

Rose had to say to the girls every day, "Look at me. We are the same."

The girls believed in their souls that they were lower, and we were higher. They believed they were worthless. At first, they believed they had no right to be in our home, or to exist in the world at all. Changing this mentality was a hard and seemingly endless job.

While I managed a lot of day to day things—like paying the rent, raising money for all the expenses of caring for the children and communicating with our supporters—Rose's priority was that of a mother, and her deepest commitment was to listen to the girls. The girls would come home from school and share everything that happened. And all day long Rose would repeat, "You can do it, you can dream. You don't need to marry while you are still a child. You can have a future. You deserve a good life and you can have one."

She said these things over and over, day after day, to all of the girls. These conversations would go on for years, and then new girls would arrive and we would have to start from the beginning with them. It was hard and frustrating and sometimes tedious and overwhelming. And yet, slowly, slowly, these seeds of human worth and the right to dream began to take root in our girls. After some time, we started to see them dreaming, saying things like, "I want to be a teacher," or, "I'd like to have my own shop." Each time we saw one of them believing in herself, or daring to voice a dream outside of what was allotted by birth, our hearts soared. Those small breakthroughs helped us deal with the challenges and keep moving forward.

Anna receiving her first doll; October, 2004.

Chapter 6
Learning to Dream

On one occasion, we were counseling the girls about having dreams for the future and asked them to write their boldest dreams on a piece of paper. We were surprised to discover a common theme: there were ten girls who dreamt of traveling to Brazil with us one day. But to go to Brazil was not so easy, even for us Brazilians. It was a long and expensive journey. But for the girls this was something huge. So we placed the topic in our prayers and let the girls dream this impossible dream.

Although the prospect was a little overwhelming, I felt compelled to work toward this dream for the girls. I called Dr. José and told him about our seemingly crazy desire to take a group of ten girls to Brazil. This trip would be more than just an opportunity to experience another culture and expand their imaginations beyond the only world they had ever known. Traveling to Brazil would give the girls a chance to grow in their leadership skills and tackle new challenges. The ten girls had formed a dance group, and we decided collectively that they would use their passion for dance to perform in cities across Brazil, sharing a message of hope.

The dream started to take on a real shape and form and, suddenly, doors began to open. Some kind friends in Brazil offered to sponsor the flights of a few girls. Initially, we contemplated taking only the girls whose flight cost had been covered. But we had made a commitment. Either all the girls of the group would go, or none would.

We began the long process of securing citizenship papers, passports and other documents. This was no easy process. Citizenship in Nepal had to be given by the father, which posed a problem for any girl who didn't have a father who was willing to vouch for her. Our girls became discouraged. But then, in September of that year, Raquel—who had one of the most difficult cases because her father had disappeared—was successful in obtaining citizenship. She managed to get a distant grandfather to help her. This fired up the other girls as they each proceeded down their own long journey toward citizenship and a passport.

But documentation was only one part of the puzzle. In December, we were forced to admit that we would not have enough money to travel as soon as we had hoped. We talked with the girls, telling them we needed to postpone the trip by one year, allowing more time to get money and visas. But they refused to accept this decision. They continued hoping and praying for a miracle. The girls had a very simple faith, pure and unquestioning. Because of this, things seemed to happen more easily for them. They taught us a lot about living by faith in a simple way. They believed, and things happened.

One night in January, Dr. José could not sleep. He felt God speak to his heart, "People are more important than things." Moved by this, he did some calculations and arrived at the conclusion that the Honda Civic parked in his garage would cover the better part of our girls' trip expenses. He called me in Nepal. He also sent an email with the message, "People are more important than things. God will provide."

That email fell like a joy bomb in our midst. I had already given up, but suddenly the dream to go to Brazil was reignited.

Even with this new motivation, we still doubted—would this trip really be possible? Would there be time? The ongoing struggles of obtaining citizenship and passports were truly arduous. In addition to the 10 girls in the dance group, we also decided to take Anna with us so that she could have her foot operated on and receive a prosthetic. In faith, we bought all the plane tickets. Then, the passports started showing up, one by one, just in time.

But the biggest problem did not end up being money, citizenship or passports. The biggest problem came from the false accusations placed upon us by unkind people who wanted to steal the girls' joy and dignity. These people used whatever lies they could think of to try and keep the girls from leaving the country. First, they accused us—to the government of Nepal—of being child traffickers in Brazil! This caused us trouble enough, but the most harmful accusation was even more personal: These people insisted that the girls should not be entitled to go to Brazil because they were street children, with no professional dance qualifications, and, "Who would want to see girls like that?"

Until Rose and I were officially proven innocent, the Nepali government was afraid to let the girls leave the country with us, and imposed serious restrictions on our travel. I asked God to send an "angel" who would help us find a solution.

We were getting worn out on several fronts: 1) Trying to prove that we were not child traffickers; 2) facing threats of prison and deportation; 3) keeping the girls from internalizing the nasty things people were saying about them.

One day, as I was heading home from a Nepali government office feeling quite discouraged, I happened to see Ms. Indira Rana, a famous Nepali social activist. I sensed she was the angel I had prayed for, so I approached her and explained our situation. She kindly agreed to help us. Almost as soon as she involved herself in the process, we were freed up by the Nepali government to take the girls to Brazil.

Three days before our departure, Nepali Immigration released me from the accusation of having an illegal visa and trafficking children. (They had received commendation from the Brazilian justice system testifying to our innocence.) Now I was free to leave the country. They also said I was welcome to return—very kind of them.

As if all of this wasn't enough, the country of Nepal went into a complete crisis just days before we were supposed to leave. There were protests in the streets against the monarchy and curfews were imposed. With tires burning on the street corners and bombs exploding, we couldn't see how we would make it out. But our girls' dream could not be extinguished, so we persevered.

On April 9th, 2006, we put our suitcases on top of our old van and left for the airport; myself, Rose, David and eleven Nepali girls. To avoid having the van attacked and burned, we wrote in great big red letters all around the vehicle, "Going to the airport." But what would have been more accurate was, "A big happy family, going to live out our dreams together."

I had many fears at that point, and the girls did too. I worried there would be more false accusations upon departure, problems at check-in or at immigration. But thankfully, everything went smoothly. The police helped us in the line outside the airport and we passed through every checkpoint with no further issues. During take off, we could feel the girls' excitement for their first flight.

After many hours of travel and several transfers, we finally landed in Brazil. As the plane touched down in Sao Paulo, Rose leaned over and said, "Start dreaming another dream, because God has fulfilled this one."

From Sao Paulo we flew to Goiania where we were greeted at the airport with a welcome party so over the top and loud that it began to annoy the airport security. I had dreamt about this arrival, thinking, "These are my people, my city and my territory."

I am not from the city of Goiania, but it was MCM's base and the home of many dear friends, so it always felt like our home, too. We were in the midst of those who loved us, finally able to share our homeland, our families and our friends with our new family of Nepali girls.

In every city we visited, the girls were shown kindness and respect. In Brasília, the capital, the girls were honored as "Nepali princesses in Brazil" as they performed in front of government officials at the Esplanada government buildings. In my hometown state of Paraná, they were praised as "children who bring honor to the city."

The girls danced and spoke at large venues for up to 4,000 people and small venues of 100 people or less. They gave presentations in churches and schools, on TV channels and radio stations, and even in a nursing home. Wherever we went, we shared compassion, dreams and hope. We did not speak about money or difficulties or ask for donations. We just shared that there is hope and we must never stop dreaming and working for justice.

Saili played guitar and sang for thousands of people, bringing joy to everyone who heard her. Brazilians were moved to hear her singing in Portuguese, accompanied by the other girls. I had told Saili we would buy her a new guitar in Brazil. But after the first place she played, someone gave her a guitar—expensive, new and valuable. How she loved that gift!

I always wondered if Saili had any experience with guitar before she came to live with us, but it was only now, in Brazil, that I had the courage to ask her about it. She said, "Yes." Now it made sense how easily she performed the songs. After all, she had already played somewhere before.

Then I asked where she had played, and she explained, "Uncle, I had never laid hands on a guitar. The contact was solely visual. In the restaurant where I worked, a young man played guitar for the customers. But I wasn't worthy of getting close to the guitar. I never even touched a finger to one of his guitars. I just watched from afar and dreamed that one day I would play."

We traveled close to 17,000 kilometers around Brazil in a van at a leisurely pace. We would stop to drink juice and eat ice cream, and we didn't worry much about the time. Wherever we went, we ate in good places. We ate many sandwiches and pizzas, dozens of boxes of chocolate and lots of ice cream and churrasco (world-famous Brazilian steak). We went out shopping and visited parks and soccer stadiums. We went to Foz do Iguaçu, where the girls cried as they saw the Iguazu Falls (the largest system of waterfalls in the world). But the most unforgettable moment came in Caioba, when the girls saw the ocean for the first time.

And of course, there was Anna's dream too. We found a doctor who agreed to see her and review the case of her deformed foot. Everyone at the hospital was extremely kind. She was treated with much love, which made her feel confident about having the surgery. When I went to pay the bill, the balance was $0. The doctors didn't charge anything! The hospital charged only some minimum fee, which other good souls generously took care of.

Then, after a brief period of recovery, Anna got an orthopedic shoe. But I wasn't happy with this. Her dream was a shiny, new foot. So we found a clinic that made perfect prosthetic feet from silicone with carbon fiber in the base. It looked like a scene from a movie, with cut-off hands and feet painted the color of the customer's skin. For Anna, the prosthetic wasn't merely a question of aesthetics. It was a necessity. A proper foot would give her body the balance it needed to avoid future spinal problems.

A few days before we were scheduled to return to Nepal, I was waiting at the airport for Rose and Anna to arrive from their short trip to pick up the prosthetic. One of the happiest moments of my life was seeing Anna walk off that plane, taking firm, confident steps on her new foot. Her Brazilian father gave thanks in tears.

With the time to leave Brazil drawing near, a cloud of melancholy came over the group. The girls knew they would soon be leaving a place of support and love and returning to a country where they would continue to suffer questioning and hostility because of their backgrounds. The last leg of the trip was more somber than the previous drives. But the girls knew their dream had been fulfilled. There was gratitude in all of our hearts.

At home in Nepal there was a period of readjustment. It wasn't easy for the girls to get back into their routines and classwork. They remembered Brazil almost constantly, and would say in Portuguese with a Nepali accent, "Homesick, homesick."

The impact of the love and support of hundreds of Brazilians did a lot of good for their souls. They returned with a new energy and motivation, conscious of the mission and challenge ahead of them. Our mission had now become theirs. They urgently wanted to go into the streets and red light areas of Nepal and India, rescuing new girls for our homes and teaching them that it is possible to dream, and that there is hope.

The dance group performing in Brazil.

Seeing the ocean for the first time; April, 2006.

Chapter 7
The Dream Crosses New Borders

Several months before our big trip to Brazil, Dr. José had forwarded me an article from Readers' Digest that talked about the problem of child sex trafficking in Cambodia. Rose and I had been working in Nepal for about five years at this point. I thought to myself, "What does Cambodia have to do with me? I am in Nepal, and surely I have enough work to do here."

However, I couldn't deny that the article was astonishing. It explained that there were an estimated 20,000 girls in sexual exploitation in the Cambodian capital of Phnom Penh alone (this was in 2005). Their average age was 15, but there was also a thriving market for very small girls as young as five or six.

In the following months I forgot about the article. But as time went on, I began thinking about Cambodia more and more. Part of me wanted to go there to see if what the article said was really true, while another part of me thought, "Why do I need to get involved in Cambodia? Surely there must be other people there doing the same work as us." But the more I tried to avoid it, the more Cambodia kept invading my thoughts.

During our time in Brazil with the girls, we attended one conference in particular where I was feeling quite sure of myself. Most of the people at an event like this were not spending their lives serving in foreign countries. This was not my case—I was giving my life to serve the children of Nepal—so I felt pretty comfortable. This feeling did not last very long, because the band leading the music soon began to sing,

How many things have I done for my own pleasure?
    I have sought after my own desires
While there are so many anxious people...
    And to You, Lord, I say yes again.
Here am I. Send me where you want to.[2]

As soon as I heard these words, Cambodia echoed in my heart. I saw that, even though I was working hard in Nepal, I needed to say "yes" again, this time to help the abused children of Cambodia. I decided I would go, even if it meant using up the few resources I had.

When we returned to Nepal I made my plan to visit Cambodia. Now that I was sure of my decision I couldn't get there fast enough. But I would have to wait. My plan was delayed by a kidney crisis that resulted in surgery and an infection that almost took my life. Nevertheless, I was set on going. After several weeks of recovery, I was on my way to Cambodia, against the recommendations of my doctors.

Upon arrival in Phnom Penh, I found a hotel, got settled and took a shower. As I prepared to go out and acquaint myself with

---

2 Asaph Borba, "Eis-me-Aqui," *Jubileu 25 Anos*, 2001.

the city, I noticed something curious on the nightstand: there was an ad offering young girls for sexual encounters. I had never seen anything so explicit.

When I left the hotel, I saw dozens of tuk-tuks (motorcycle taxis that pull a type of carriage in which the passenger sits). Several came in my direction. I was trying to decide which to take when I noticed one of the drivers smiling at me, so I decided this would be my ride. He asked for $5 to take me to any point in the city. As we drove around the capital stopping at various temples and tourist spots, I noticed his genuine concern that I not be robbed. He took care of my backpack, and this made me trust him.

The most sobering stop of the day was when we visited the Killing Fields—the place where over two million Cambodians had been murdered under the regime of Pol Pot and the Khmer Rouge. I felt tremendous compassion and sorrow for this nation that had suffered so much in such a recent past.

At the end of an exhausting day in the Southeast Asian heat, my driver took me back to the hotel. I tried to talk with him about child sex trafficking, but he did not speak very much English, so our conversation did not go very far. In front of the hotel, an agent approached us. He did speak English well, and suggested I have an encounter with some girls. My driver seemed to resist the dialogue with this other Cambodian man, but I accepted the proposal. I wanted to go to a red light area and see if there really were children there.

What happened next was the most shocking experience of my life. We arrived at a building in the red light area near downtown. Another agent, who was also now serving as my translator, led me to a room where I counted fourteen plastic chairs placed in a circle. My driver stayed outside with my backpack. A lady shouted something in the Khmer language and I soon noticed a familiar sound, one that I heard all the time in my own house—the sound of many children descending a staircase.

Eight girls entered the room. Two were young adults. Another two were adolescents. Four of them, however, were small children, younger than eleven. I understood immediately the purpose of the chairs. They were there so the girls could be introduced to me. I was expected to choose one or more of them for a sexual encounter. The agent who had been translating for me, presumably the manager of the place, began to speak in English about the youth and beauty of the girls seated in front of me.

I did not move. I was familiar with the methods of child sex trafficking and this scene should not have been so surprising, but still I had no words. I never imagined I would face this situation. The agent insisted I choose one of the girls, but I remained silent, even though I feared this could be interpreted as displeasure on my part. The girls all looked either frightened or numb.

I knew that I only had a few minutes here. It took all my self control to keep from crying. But I had to do something. I tried to look deeply into each of their eyes. My hope was that, through this gesture, I might convey, "I am not here to exploit you. I see your humanity. You are not alone. God sees and loves you, and there are people, like me, who want to help." But I could not say it out loud. I did not know how to speak their language. And there was no use in saying it in English, because, surely, the agent would not translate this sentiment for me. Not to mention that he might see me as a threat to his business.

In the girls' eyes I saw unimaginable suffering and a complete lack of dreams and hope. I saw the pain of humiliation.

As I left the building, I noticed the manager complaining to my driver because I had not chosen any of the girls.

I felt sick to my stomach. On the way back to the hotel I asked the driver to stop and I did, in fact, vomit. Seeing that I was not well, he kindly helped me. I began to cry uncontrollably. We stopped at a café and asked for an espresso. I tried to drink it, but I could not stop shaking. Next, I went to a cyber-café to write to Rose and some friends. Rose replied to the message saying that everyone was shocked and deeply affected.

I decided then and there that I would do something to help the trafficked children of Cambodia—even spend my last cent if necessary. I knew many people were working and helping in that region, but clearly more help was needed. I stayed in Phnom Penh a few more days before returning to Nepal, each day becoming more and more convinced that I had to say "yes" to Cambodia.

Several months later, I returned to Cambodia with the goal of finding a house to rent. Lucas (who had been leading our Home 2 with his wife Sheyla), Lucas' son, and a friend from the USA came with me. We learned that Phnom Penh had 18 rescue shelters for trafficked girls, but there were not many of these homes in the north of the country. Several people suggested we look into establishing our home in Siem Reap—a tourist city, home to the famous Angkor Wat temples. So we made our way six hours north to see for ourselves. Standing in front of the huge temples, I felt a deep sense of recognition, as if I had been there before. I decided that Siem Reap would be the site of our first home in Cambodia.

Back in Nepal, we gathered our girls together and talked about the risks of opening another house, especially one outside of Nepal. We talked about the potential lack of provisions we might face if we stretched our limited resources to another country, and how that could affect them. They decided, voluntarily, that it was worth the risk. We had to have faith that there would be enough for the homes in both Nepal and Cambodia. The only question remaining was: who would help lead this new home in another country?

A few years earlier, while I was visiting the USA, Rose had called me to say that Muna, a girl from the Dalit (once called "untouchable") caste kept knocking on our gate, asking for a chance to live in our home so she could go to school. But our home was already more than full. Rose continued bringing up Muna in the days that followed, and I continued to resist. Muna did not fit the profile of girls we had come to Nepal to serve, and our resources were already stretched thin.

A few weeks later, I was flying back from the USA to Nepal, my heart filled with gratitude. I was returning with fifteen suitcases full of clothes and toys for our children, as well as generous financial donations that would cover our expenses for several months. I had also been given enough funds to buy a van, which we desperately needed.

I wondered what I should do to show my gratitude. The memory of Rose's words about Muna and her persistent request for help pierced my mind like an arrow. I decided that we needed to take this child in and give her the opportunity she sought for an education and a safe place to live. When I told Rose of my change of heart, she vibrated with joy. She had known all along that this was the right path.

Now, when we needed a Nepali volunteer to go to Cambodia for an extended time, Muna stepped forward. For the girl who knocked on the door of our house, and who kept knocking on more closed doors, the doors of the world opened up.

In May of 2007, I traveled to Cambodia for the third time in eight months. This time we brought Muna and a Brazilian woman named Rosiane. We rented a house, furnished it and bought beds. In this simple manner, we set up our first Cambodian home for girls in Siem Reap. Muna worked there for eight months. She had been considered by many to be a lesser person because she came from a low caste, but her service and effectiveness in Cambodia proved to everyone that she was a person of great integrity and worth.

Many wonderful people provided support, which allowed us to set up the house quickly and not fall into debt. Dr. José helped pay for plane tickets and other expenses. Luz das Nações (Light of the Nations), my church in Brazil led by Luiz (aka Luigi) Riccioppo, provided all the furniture for the house. Rosiane and Muna took care of the documents to legalize the work with the government of Cambodia. And so, the first safe home was established in Siem Reap.

Later, a couple named Lucas and Laurine came to help run the home, followed by another family who looked after it for some time. During these first few years the work had its ups and downs, but it survived.

Several years later, Thiago and Patricia, another couple from Brazil, came to live permanently in Cambodia and oversee the operation of the homes there. The work in Siem Reap has been flourishing under their leadership, and today they are running three homes full of 70 children, using the Apple model of family-style care and healing.

The issue of child trafficking in Cambodia has its own unique challenges. While it may look different from Nepal in some ways, the same truth can be found, regardless of the country and culture: When children are shown their dignity and value in a loving, family environment, there's no evil in the world that can hold back their dreams.

*Signing a Memorandum of Understanding
with the Cambodia government; 2008.*

*Silvio with the present-day Cambodia Director,
Thiago; March, 2024.*

Chapter 8
Asha

In early 2006, Rose and I drove out to a remote village near the China-Tibet border to see the famous Sino-Nepal Friendship Bridge. While there, we took the opportunity to visit a friend, Kaji, who pastored a church in the area. When we arrived in the village, we met his congregation, a small group of people who seemed famished and desperate. In the group was a boy whose body was deformed from sickness. We offered to help by taking him to the capital and paying for his medical treatment.

The caretaker of this little congregation then told us about the case of a tiny baby girl, only two months old, living in a nearby village. The baby's mother had died in childbirth, so she was being cared for by her grandmother. But the grandmother would not be able to care for her much longer. The baby's one-year-old sister had already died due to lack of food and harsh conditions. The church caretaker asked us if we could shelter this little baby in our home.

I was reluctant because The Apple of God's Eyes didn't generally take in babies. But Rose was interested in the case. She had been praying for a baby girl and heard God speak to her that He "would bring her to our gate." I argued that this remote village was not exactly the gate of our house.

On the return trip to Kathmandu, we wrestled with what decision to make about sheltering this little baby. The discussion became quite heated. Rose insisted we take in the baby. I could accept that we would do this as an organization, but Rose wanted something more—she wanted us to adopt the girl as our own child. This shocked me a bit. Nepal had confusing adoption laws that were difficult to interpret and full of contradictions. We also did not have permanent visas at that time. Beyond these difficulties, we had already lived through a traumatic experience caring for a baby back in Brazil (before we had adopted David). We fostered him for nine months and were trying to adopt him, but then his biological mother recovered from her troubles and the judge decided to put the baby back into the mother's care.

Even with all these factors, no argument could convince Rose to change her mind. By the end of the seven hour drive, we decided we would take responsibility for this tiny person. While plans were made for the church caretaker to bring the baby to us in Kathmandu in the next few days, I had to make a quick trip to India. I was waiting at the New Delhi airport to return home when Rose called to tell me that the baby was arriving at our house that very minute.

When I walked into our bedroom at midnight, I saw at the side of my bed a crib improvised from a small sofa. In it lay a tiny, dark-skinned baby girl with a triangular face. She was so small she looked like she might break if we held her. At two months old, she weighed only six pounds, three ounces—the weight of a newborn. Despite her small size and malnutrition, her gaze was steady. She looked directly into my eyes. At that moment, I felt an irresistible love being born, but I did not say anything to Rose. She still thought I was against the baby being there. The child's name was Bhudimaya, which in Nepali means "wise love" or "born on Wednesday", but Rose had already chosen another name months ago. She had decided that the next girl to come into our home needing a name would be called Asha, which means "hope".

Days passed. The tiny baby would cry faintly with her small, hoarse voice. Lying beside her on the bed, that sound was music to my ears. Rose would hurry to take care of her, fearing that the crying would annoy me.

The following weeks were tense. We were in the middle of arranging all the details for the trip to Brazil with the dance group, and at the same time taking care of a baby who was very ill with pneumonia and malnutrition.

Rose spent days on end in different hospitals with different doctors. Many days, it looked like Asha would not survive. I suffered to see Rose so attached to the little baby and started worrying how she would cope if the baby did not survive. More than this, I already loved Asha deeply. I just had not admitted it yet.

Sheyla helped Rose care for Asha while everyone worked toward the girls' trip to Brazil. Then, everything seemed to fall apart as we faced problem after problem with Nepali Immigration. In the middle of it all, I could hear God telling me, "Do not fear. There is hope in your lives." I didn't connect the word hope with the name of the baby at first. A few days later, I suddenly saw the correlation: the hope that God had ministered to my heart was Asha.

While we traveled to Brazil with the girls, Asha stayed with her "grandparents", Sheyla and Lucas. Separated by oceans, we were tortured in our souls about Asha's health. We talked about her wherever we went, showing off pictures of how she arrived at our house and how she was getting strong and smiling. She brought hope wherever we mentioned her name. I finally admitted to Rose that I had loved Asha since the first minute I saw her. Perhaps I had even loved her from the first moment I heard her life spoken of.

When we began the adoption process, we had no idea we were entering the biggest fight of our lives. At that exact time, Nepal had closed international adoption and, to make matters worse, Brazil did not have an embassy in Nepal, only an honorary consulate.

We hired a good lawyer to help us with the adoption process. But each time we approached the Nepalese government something else had changed in the laws. Nepal had signed a convention that disallowed adoptions for people who were already in touch with a specific child. Adoption was much easier if you didn't know the child before beginning the process, but some exceptions were being allowed. Another law forbade exceptions, as these laws had been created to curb fraud or even child trafficking in the name of adoption. The laws were intended to prevent Nepali children from being put up for adoption when there was a relative able to care for them.

As for our little Asha, nobody seemed to understand that we had come to know her as she lay dying. We tried asking some government orphanages to keep her temporarily while we pursued legal adoption, but none accepted. If she wasn't properly cared for, she could become sick again, and possibly die. In the process of caring for her, we had fallen in love with her. As soon as she had been old enough to recognize family members, it was only us in her sight.

ASHA

The years kept passing, government officials kept changing and we kept having to retell our story. Over and over we had to explain why Asha was with us and not in an orphanage. Many Nepalese orphanages were notorious for participating in unethical adoptions—some for financial gain.[3] There were even some organizations fighting to completely outlaw adoption in Nepal. People made movies and gave speeches against it, with no attention or investigation given to genuine cases such as Asha's. I cannot even express how distressing it was, with so much controversy, endless bureaucracy and no one listening to us.

As the months of waiting turned into years, we continued to raise Asha in our home as our own daughter. She was growing up and beginning to have an understanding of life. Because she had no passport, and was not legally our child, she couldn't make any international trips with us. Whenever she came to the airport with us to pick someone up, she asked why she couldn't travel, and we would have to explain that she didn't have the legal papers. Perhaps she sensed there was something unsettled and unsure about the situation, and that made her worried.

Rose went almost six years without making any trips. I reduced my travel as much as I could, only leaving for a few weeks at a time for essential trips. At one point, Rose became critically ill and had to be taken to Thailand for treatment. Even then, Asha had to stay behind.

---

[3] Because of this issue, when we registered Nepalese Home, we strictly said that it was *not* for the purpose of adoptions or providing an orphanage for parentless kids. Instead, its purpose was to provide shelter and education for survivors and kids at risk of exploitation, for as long as they needed. We have always worked to reintegrate kids with their families when they were ready to stand on their own feet.

But we believed the promise of God written in Hebrews 10:35-38, which talks about the promise to come, saying we have to do a few things:

To persevere after doing the will of God.

To be patient.

To keep faith.

Such a promise warmed our hearts, as it concludes with, "You will receive what He has promised." We believed that, just like the promise that God will come, so also for all His promises. We need to persevere, be patient and have faith.

Every time we felt despairing, every time our lawyer came with bad news or the government shut the door in our faces, God's promise warmed our hearts.

Asha was fascinated with travel and airplanes. One day I brought home a pink suitcase with wheels for her. She would put some clothes inside and walk in and out of the room saying, "I was in Brazil, it was hot there," or, "I was in America, and there it was snowing." She would see photos of places and our family in Brazil, or friends in America, and say, "One day I will be there!" Often, she would make Rose and I join in her pretend travel too. Asha would choose a seat in the plane for us and we had to imagine we were eating airplane food. I taught her about the check-in processes and everything related to flying.

One afternoon, Asha heard Rose talking on the phone to her father in Brazil. He was saying that Rose's Grandma (who raised her) was very sick in intensive care and might pass away at any moment. Rose very sadly explained that she couldn't go to Brazil to say goodbye because Asha had no papers to travel, and she would not leave her. Hearing this, Asha said to Rose, "Mama, you can go to Brazil to see your sick grandmother, Asha [she spoke of herself in the third person] doesn't have papers and will stay behind. No problem, go!"

Rose pulled Asha into her arms and said, "Look into my eyes. I have an alliance with you and I won't go to Brazil without you."

After a few days, to our surprise, Grandma moved out of the ICU, and was soon well enough to leave the hospital.

In May 2011, I got a phone call from someone at the Brazilian Consulate in Nepal—but it was not about our adoption process. He said there was a Brazilian citizen who had had some kind of breakdown, broken things in his hotel, been arrested and was now refusing to speak in English to the local authorities (or maybe he did not know how to speak English). The incident had taken place near our house, so the consulate was calling to see if we could help.

We went to the local police station where the Brazilian man was in custody. He was hurt and bleeding from all the glass he had broken at the hotel. At first, he refused to talk to me because I wasn't from the consulate. The police asked me to make reports in English and Portuguese saying they were giving him back his passport, cash and other valuables. As I was about to leave, the guy finally wanted to speak with me. I agreed to go with the police officers to take him to get medical attention. The hospital was so full that some people in the emergency room had already died while waiting.

Though I didn't know this guy, I stayed right by his side, acting as his translator and doing what I could to make sure he was taken care of. The next day he was admitted to the psychiatric ward. The consulate staff were very helpful every step of the way, also working to protect this Brazilian citizen who was in the middle of an emotional crisis. His drug tests came back clean. It seemed that his breakdown had been caused by stress.

The next day Rose was able to contact the man's wife, and after another day she arrived in Nepal with their baby and another friend to retrieve him. Nepal was totally foreign to her, so we had her stay in our home with us. She needed support and kindness in such an upsetting situation. After a couple days, the guy was well enough to be discharged from the hospital. Meanwhile, the Brazilian Consulate arranged what was needed to help him to return home safely.

After that strange storm, our lives got back into a normal routine. A few weeks later, the Brazilian Consul, Mr. Binay Srestha, invited me for lunch to express their gratitude. We saw no connection between the situation of the distressed man and our adoption case. Our motivation to help had been purely humanitarian, with no thought that it could benefit us. But soon after the incident, our adoption process started moving forward.

When the Nepalese Government requested a recommendation letter, we asked the Brazilian Consulate for a single line. But to honor us—and knowing we had been suffering on account of our daughter for a very long time—Mr. Srestha wrote an entire letter, strongly commending us to the Nepalese Government, saying that we were good people and had done everything in a legal way to adopt Asha.

The process was now ready to go through the government matching committee. They would analyze Asha's adoption process and decide whether to approve it or not. We had heard scary things about this committee. We had heard that, because of pressure from organizations working against adoptions, the committee generally didn't approve cases where children were already living with the prospective parents. Instead, they would deny the adoption and give the child to another couple, causing terrible suffering to both the child and the prospective parents. We didn't know how true these stories were, but it was terrifying to hear.

When bad thoughts and anxiety came, we diffused our worry by remembering the words of God: "Persevere...you will receive what He has promised." These words helped us hold on to hope and kept us from being destroyed by the waiting and the fear.

Then, at 8:32 p.m. on August 25th, 2011, we got a phone call from one of our team members on our secondary number. She told us that our lawyer had been desperately trying to reach us, but our main line had been busy for a long time. When he couldn't get through to us, he called her. We immediately ended our call on the other line and Rose called the lawyer. Rose began to shout and celebrate with tears and laughter all at once, so I knew something good must have happened. I had to take the phone from her because she was crying so hard she couldn't speak. Our lawyer told me that the matching committee had made their decision. We would be allowed to adopt Asha.

No longer just the daughter of our hearts, now at last Asha would be our legal daughter too. The girls brought out the guitar to sing and celebrate. They wanted to go out for dinner but we were exhausted from all the emotions, so we celebrated at home, then fell into bed.

Now that the main fight was won, we still had to navigate the process of getting Asha a passport and Brazilian visa. But these remaining hurdles seemed small in comparison. Even the 6.0 earthquake that struck Nepal as we prepared our trip could not shake our joy.

One month after the life-changing phone call, Asha's passport arrived. That very evening she fulfilled her dream of going inside the airport. Our Nepali girls shouted with happiness outside as Asha proudly rolled her pink suitcase into the departures area, feeling her own worth and dignity. Moments later she completed her check-in process—something she had pretended to do a hundred times.

We boarded our first flight, and Asha got to enjoy being served by flight attendants for real. After many long hours enjoying each moment of each flight, the captain announced, "Ladies and gentlemen please fasten your seat belts as we are starting our descent to Sao Paulo, Brazil." I was crying and Rose was too. Asha traveled to many places on that first trip to Brazil, at last meeting the people and seeing the places she had known only as photos. She was able to meet her great grandma (Rose's grandmother) and receive a blessing from her. It seemed that she had held on through her sickness just long enough to meet Asha, as she passed away a few weeks after we got back to Nepal.

We remained in touch with Asha's blood family, including the aunt who gave breast milk for her, trying to keep her alive when she was first born. We have done our best to care for that village and those people. We respect them and are grateful to them as Asha's people.

The first time we went back to the village with Asha, when she was six years old and we had just gotten her adoption papers, the entire village walked out to meet us, weeping for joy. They were amazed and astonished to see Asha so healthy. She had been close to death the last time they saw her. They told us that it wasn't only Asha who got blessed, the whole village got blessed because of her. Today, as a family we continue to stay connected with Asha's village. Her grandmother, who is now 89 years old, has faced various health challenges and ended up moving in with us. It's a joy to hear her having conversations with the Bollywood movies and Nepalese TV shows she watches from our couch. Seeing Asha continue her relationship with her and help care for her as she ages has been a gift to our family.

Persevere. You will receive what He has promised.

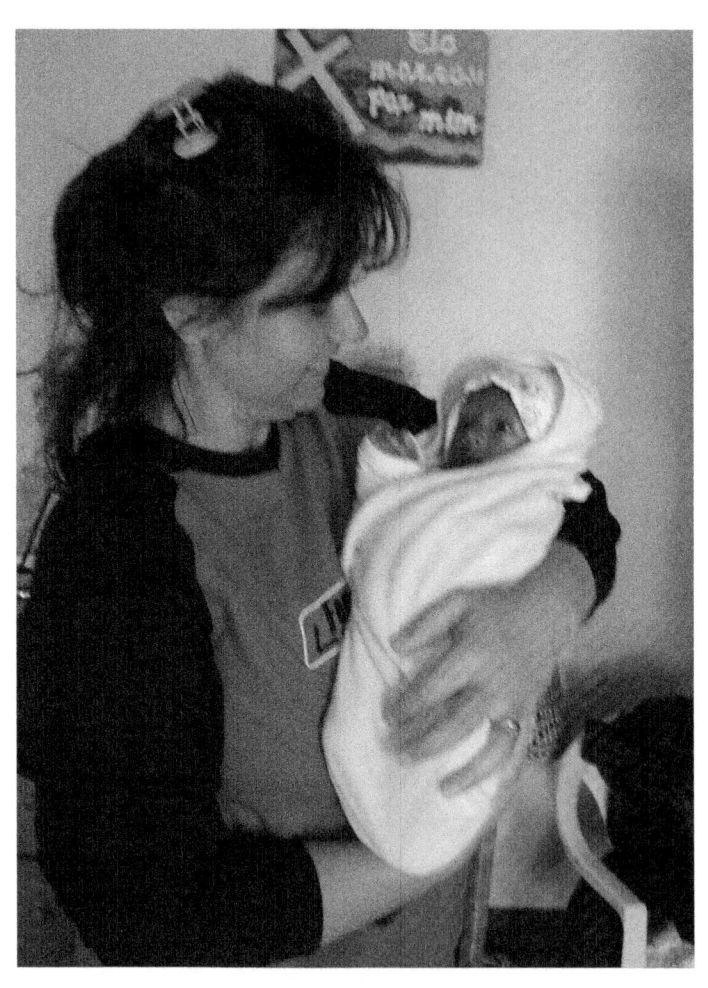

Baby Asha; March, 2006.

Asha's sweet sixteen; 2022.

Chapter 9
Embracing Change

The Brothers

Often, when we were out in the city with our girls, we would see their brothers living on the streets. Sometimes we would see a street boy from a bus window, and one of the girls would say, "Oh, that's my brother," and ask to stop and talk with them. These were small boys, as young as seven. One girl's brother died of pneumonia related to drug use.

Several times we tried to put one of these little brothers, Ram, into a boys home run by a friend of ours. We gave some monthly support for him and brought a mattress and clothes for him. But after a few days he ran away and came to our Home 1. He wanted to be close to his sister.

Around this time, we had a guest visiting from Brazil who thought I was too liberal in the way we operated our home with the girls, how they dressed and so on. He saw Ram hanging around and said, "See that boy? Aren't you afraid, having that boy here? He could abuse your girls."

Many times I made my choices through careful consideration and how I felt God directing me. I followed my beliefs and values and did things because they were right. But I confess, sometimes I made decisions out of reaction to people's criticism or accusations. Because of what that guy said, I took Ram back to our friend's home for boys. I actually wanted him to stay with us, near his sister. I wasn't doing this by conviction. I was doing it because I was afraid I would be blamed if something bad did happen.

Then, a good friend, Eber Rodrigues (Dr. José's son), came to visit from Brazil and I asked him, "What do you see in that boy?"

He said, "I see a child of God, a good boy."

"You don't see an abuser, a possible danger to our girls?" I asked.

He said, "No, he is just a kid. He wants to be near his sister." I asked him if he would support us in starting a home for boys, and he agreed to help.

Kristina, one of the girls in our home, was always smiling, always lifting others up. At one point, her mother came to visit, bringing a little boy of about three years old. When her mother left, Kristina was sad for many days. I tried to ask her what was going on, but she wouldn't tell me. She said everything was fine, but I knew it was not fine.

Promila had the gift of being able to pull anything out of anyone, so I asked her to talk to Kristina. The next day she came to me and said, "I found out what's wrong, but you can't tell Kristina I told you. She made me promise not to tell you."

Kristina's mother had told her she was going to put her little brother up for adoption. Because Kristina and her sisters were living with us, they weren't producing money for their family anymore, so their mother had no money to feed the boy. Kristina heard that if he was adopted, he would be sent to some foreign country, probably Spain. She loved her brother, so this made her very sad.

She begged her mother not to do it, but she said it was already in progress. Giving kids up for adoption was easy back then. Some orphanages were selling kids for adoption, getting around 6,000 euros per child. (This is why Asha's adoption was so difficult, because the whole country was under accusation.)

I went to the door of her room and said, "Kristina, now I know why you are sad, because of your brother. Let's get your little brother, let's bring him here."

She said, "Oh Uncle, I know it's not possible. This is a project for girls, the laws and everything say it's just for girls."

I said, "Let's forget the laws, the rules. My duty is to make you happy. Yes, we had a vision to help girls in the beginning, but now you are my daughter and my main duty is to make you happy. Bringing your brother will make you happy. If you promise to help look after him, we can bring him tomorrow."

That little boy officially became a member of our family, the first boy in the project. Then we got another little boy named Daniel, and then the boys started to multiply. Soon, we had eight boys. At first we put them in a section of Lucas and Sheyla's House, and then we opened our Boy's Home officially in 2008. The tiny ones remained in Home 1, with their mothers or sisters.

The boys that came to us over the years included boys whose sisters had been trafficked, boys facing neglect and abuse in their homes, and boys who, had they not been removed from their homes, would have been coerced into becoming traffickers like the other young men in their villages, following their parents "business".

One spring, the girls told us, "It's Brothers Day and we need to go bless our brothers." We didn't know what Brothers Day was. They explained that it's a holiday to celebrate the bond between brothers and sisters, where sisters honor their brothers by tying string bracelets on their brothers' wrists. In more recent times, the brothers also do this for their sisters. Sarada, our nurse, convinced us that she should organize a Brothers Day event at the home. She made special foods, said prayers, put a flower garland on me and ceremonially made me her brother. People took photos of us on our digital camera. It was a beautiful and honoring experience.

The next day I had to go to immigration to renew my visa. But I was having some difficulties—they didn't want to give it to me. While waiting, I was looking at the pictures on my camera. The immigration guy came and looked over my shoulder and saw the Brothers' Day photos. He said, "Who is that girl? She is putting tikka on you, putting mala and katha around your neck. She made you her brother."

He was so impressed by this that he told his boss, "Give this guy his visa, he is one of our own."

The next year, now that we understood Brothers' Day, we knew we had to bring the girls' brothers into the homes to celebrate. Some had lost brothers to glue-sniffing, or diseases from living on the streets, but some still had living brothers. That day, the team from MCM was with us. They were quite conservative, so I was worried they might criticize me for celebrating a Hindu festival. I thought I should explain the situation to Dr. José. But when he saw the girls showing love to their brothers, he saw their hearts and got emotional. He said, "Silvio, this is not about any religion. This is about God. This is about love. Sisters and brothers honoring each other, reconciliation, forgiveness. Even if they have been fighting all year. Reconciliation is from God. Love is from God."

Moving Out

Later that year, Rose became deathly ill. She had a parasite in her liver and we had to take her to Thailand for treatment. After her surgery, Rose needed peace in order to recover, but there was too much noise in the house with fifty-two kids running around. After eight years of living in the home with the girls, we realized that it was time for us to move out.

Our son David was getting bigger. He was fourteen now, and sometimes when he was playing with the girls, wrestling with them like brother and sisters, we worried that someone would take it the wrong way. Also, our desire was to continue giving more leadership to the Nepali people, not to remain in charge forever. We strongly believed in this approach.

For all these reasons, we knew it was time to move out of Home 1. But when we told the girls, their first reaction was that we were abandoning them. They felt so hurt. They were extremely attached to both David and Asha too. Our moving out felt like a betrayal to them. But we knew it was time, so we rented another house and started to transfer our things. Some girls helped, and some didn't. They thought we were leaving them behind. They thought they were becoming orphans again. It was hard!

But then, after a month or two, they started to enjoy their newfound freedom and independence. I asked them, "Kids, do you want us to come back and live in the house again?"

They said, "No thanks, we're fine. You can come visit once or twice in a week, we'll be okay. We are fine. Stay where you are."

They enjoyed making more decisions for themselves. When we moved out we put Muna and Eliza, two of our first generation girls, in charge. At first, we gave them the money to buy food daily. Then, we would give money for one week, and then for a whole month, for all the bills and food. They managed it all beautifully.

First Marriage Celebration

Promila was the first of our girls to marry, followed by Muna (who had helped set up the first home in Cambodia). Whenever one of the girls got married, I felt an enormous sense of hope and redemption, because we believed so strongly in family. Yes, Apple is a beautiful place, with a loving family model, but it's not exactly the same as a regular family. We are many people living together. Yes, we are a family, but we know that this is not all that people need.

When the girls got married, they were finally starting to build their own family. I told them, "As you build your family, you have the opportunity of *not* doing what your parents did. Now you can rewrite history in a good way. You have the power now to write the story. You have the opportunity to build a functional family. You have the power to do things differently."

Opening a School

In 2009, we decided to open our own school. This was a huge milestone for us, because we had always struggled with sending our kids to public schools. They constantly faced discrimination and disrespect from teachers and other kids—because they came from the villages, because they were poor and because they were often years behind in their education. Sending them to private schools had improved the situation somewhat, but there were still problems. The kids did not look forward to going to school when they knew they might be ridiculed by classmates or singled out and humiliated by the teacher.

Having our own school made it easier to incorporate girls who were repatriated from India, and others who were many years behind in their education. In our school, there were always kids of different ages and sizes in every class. No one thought anything of it, and no one was made to feel self-conscious or ashamed.

Sheyla, with her background and experience in education, spearheaded the effort. She helped create a school with high academic standards and a culture of kindness. We welcomed low income kids from the surrounding neighborhoods to study alongside the children for our homes, and gave them free or low tuition. This helped us build connections and grow our roots in the community. Thanks to the Sheyla's high standards, our students began to excel in the standardized tests given each year by the government. More importantly, our kids—even the most vulnerable and sensitive—now loved and looked forward to going to school each day. They knew that their dignity and human worth would be protected at school just as it was in the homes.

Business Experiments

Alongside all the joys and successes, of course many things failed. We were not shaped only by victories. One year, we started a carpet weaving project to provide the older girls with a way to earn an income. We thought they would enjoy it. We imagined them weaving their stories into the carpet, literally and figuratively. But that initiative didn't work well at all. The girls did not enjoy doing such tedious work. We had no idea how laborious it would actually be. Apparently carpet-weaving is mostly done by the very poorest people, because no one else wants to do it.

The carpets were heavy and it was not profitable to sell them in Brazil or the US because of the shipping cost.

Next, we tried setting up hot dog carts in the busy district of Thamel to sell to tourists. That business soon collapsed too. Then we tried a food truck selling momos (dumplings), Nepali people's most beloved food. Unfortunately, the momos were too beloved, and the girls ate all the profits!

Eventually, we were forced to admit that we weren't made for running businesses. After a string of failures, my friend Don encouraged me: "You guys are not made for business, you are made for caring for people," he said. "Focus on what you do well: healing lives."

We had been trying desperately to create a business that could help us be more self-supporting. People sometimes made comments that the work we were doing, caring for so many kids, was too expensive. These businesses were our attempt to generate some of our own income and relieve people from the burden of sending us money.

Let's be honest. It costs money to heal kids' lives. We shouldn't be wasting our time on hot dogs, rugs or momos. But still, people kept coming up with all kinds of ideas for us to generate income. Finally, we decided that those ideas were taking too much time and energy from our core mission: looking after people.

Free to Fly

In 2012, a juvenile court judge from Brazil came to visit us. She told us, "You guys are doing great. But you are getting bigger and bigger and you need to have some way for kids to move on from the homes." Our goal was to eventually restore kids back with their families, but sometimes that wasn't possible. Some kids did not have families to reconnect with, and in other cases the situation just wasn't safe, or we would try it and it didn't work.

"In Brazil we have this informal system called a republic," the judge told us. "Once kids are no longer minors, they can join together with other young people, get an apartment, and make a republic together. You can put four, five or six young people together in a flat. They share expenses for food, rent and so on. In Brazil, this system is very common for kids coming out of shelters or foster care. You could make republics for your kids, for those who are able to work outside, to live on their own. Then you can support them from a little further away, not in the Homes."

Rose loved this idea. She took what she could from the Brazilian system, from this lady, and adapted it to the context here in Nepal. We called it "Free to Fly".

We had to work hard to convince our staff. Of course, some people didn't like it. Rose insisted that we try. One of our staff expressed some concern: "You are going to lose the kids. They are going to go wild out on their own."

They thought this would be too much freedom. They wanted to maintain control, to put conditions on the kids moving out on their own. I said, "No, these are young adults, not little children, and if they are Free to Fly, they are really going to be free and live their lives in their own way. It's not freedom if we force them to do things that we think are good for them."

At first, some girls felt hurt. They felt that they were being expelled from the family. The first person to take the opportunity was Saili. "I can bring my mother, my family," she said. "I can be free, eat what I want when I want. I can be independent."

Others were inspired by Saili and decided to take the opportunity. Naturally, some got into trouble. One group we set up with everything—a new fridge and furniture—but after a few months they were fighting and it didn't work out. Some Free to Fly kids would use their salary frivolously and not pay their rent. One girl was taking a taxi home from work every day! And sometimes they came back to us, saying, "I made a mistake, please help me."

We are not perfect and we can't control people. There were many troubles starting up Free to Fly, but ultimately many kids learned how to live on their own, and were successful.[4]

---

[4] The only real measure for the success of our work, in the world's eyes, is how many children are able to transition into independence once they leave our care. Most healthy programs serving this population have a 62% success rate or lower. At the time of writing this, after 24 years of operating, The Apple of God's Eyes has about a 96% success rate of reintegration, and we've helped more than 600 individuals transition to independence through our Free to Fly program.

Asha celebrating Brothers Day.

Silvio celebrating Brothers Day.

Celebrating the wedding of Promila and Stephen; 2009.

A school assembly; 2024.

PART 2

Chapter 10
Understanding the Why and the How

Why Nepali Girls are Trafficked

I have come to understand five major factors driving the trafficking of girls in Nepal: economic pressures, cultural traditions, religious beliefs, lack of education and the low status of women.

Economic Pressures

The per capita income of Nepal is among the lowest on the planet, at just $1,336 USD a year in 2022.[5] Most Nepali people live on less than a dollar a day. In reality, the picture is even more grim than the government's numbers reveal, because a large portion of the population is unregistered.

Between 1996 and 2006 there was an armed conflict between the Nepali government and a guerrilla group called the Maoists. Besides creating years of deadly confrontations, the conflict also

---

5 https://data.worldbank.org/indicator/NY.GDP.PCAP.CD?locations=NP

increased poverty by destabilizing the economy. In many villages, the young men fled to India to avoid conscription. In addition, law enforcement resources were diverted to deal with this conflict, which meant they weren't enforcing laws against trafficking.

Nepal does not suffer from starvation. Even among the Himalayas and many mountainous areas the Nepali people know how to plant every handful of land. Even though they are able to feed themselves, many people still live in desperate poverty, just one bad crop season away from ruin, and with no opportunities to improve their lives. When they are unable to support their family, parents are sometimes driven to give up their children, or send them off to work in unknown and dangerous places.

Economic pressures are further aggravated by the dowry system. In Nepal, it is typical for parents to save money for a long time so that when their daughters marry they are able to give the groom's family a generous dowry. Sometimes the dowry is equivalent to a portion of their property. An insufficient dowry can bring immense shame on the bride's family.

But what about the poor family with more than one daughter? In those cases, the pressure surrounding dowries increases exponentially. Seeing few other options, parents will sometimes turn to selling their daughters as an alternative. However, the word "sale" is almost never used because the parents, often innocently, do not believe that is what has happened.

The main motive for selling girls always comes back to this: lack of money and opportunities. Sadly, giving children away has become normalized in many communities. Often, it is a desperate but ineffective attempt to give children a better life.

Cultural Traditions

Even though, on paper, the government has abolished the caste system, many Nepalis still live under it today. Society is divided into classes following certain customs and rules that distinguish one group from another. A person's caste is known by the last name they carry, by their job or even by the way they dress. People of lower castes generally do not have access to more important positions or professions. People of higher castes regularly humiliate or exploit the lower castes and, in some cases, higher caste men rape or exploit lower caste women and girls with no consequences. This is slowly changing, but we still see abuses in this area.

Girls from the Dalit ("untouchable") caste are at particularly high risk for trafficking because of their low status in society, and because there are few or no jobs available to them. In some castes, such as the Badi, the trafficking of girls has become their main source of income, and is completely accepted and normalized.

Some castes arrange marriages for their children when they are very young—between six and ten years old. This is a way to guarantee a future spouse. Grandparents in traditional village communities believe that a late marriage brings a curse on the family. Some girls even marry before their first menstruation. This practice of child marriage has been prohibited and condemned by the government of Nepal and by humanitarian organizations. Nonetheless, in some rural communities, it continues.

It is also a common practice in Nepal for the man to live in the city while the wife, with the children, lives in a village or in the mountains, planting small plots of land. As the years go by, more and more Nepali men are going abroad to work and earn money, leaving their family for many years at a time. In these scenarios, the women must survive without the help of their husbands, who only show up once in a while. This cultural context has created disconnection in some families and communities, facilitating the discarding of girls.

Religious Beliefs

According to the 2021 census, the population of Nepal is made up of just over 29 million inhabitants, of whom 81.1% are Hindu, 8.2% are Buddhist, 5% are Muslim and 1.8% are Christian.[6] I, myself, am a Christian. But I personally do not think a change in religion would solve the problem of the trafficking of girls in Nepal. Trafficking also occurs in majority Christian countries.

In some branches of Hinduism the concept of karma is highly influential. People believe that if you suffer, you will be perfected. Even though this concept is not found in the sacred books of Hinduism it has become attached to the religion, and has shaped the lives of many Hindus. Applying the concept of karma to the trafficking of girls, some people believe that if a girl is in forced prostitution, it is because she really needs to go through that situation, and she is merely getting what she deserves for her misdeeds in a previous lifetime. I have heard this belief expressed by some influential people here in the Himalayas. But I also have Hindu friends, people very devoted to their religion, who think differently and help many people.

---

6 Government of Nepal National Statistics Office, *National Population and Housing Census 2021*

Lack of Education

The illiteracy level in Nepal is very high. In the capital and other larger cities, people have access to good schools and higher education. But the majority of Nepalis, living in rural areas, have not had access to a good education. This is especially true for the older generation. This makes it easy for traffickers to trick parents and girls with grand promises of a more prosperous life in India.

Girls who are not in school are much more likely to be trafficked, or to go willingly in search of work. Girls and boys without education have few options for earning a living outside of relentless physical labor on a family farm, going abroad for domestic work or being forced or coerced into sexual exploitation.

The Low Status of Women

Discrimination against women is a problem all over the world. However, the issues facing women in Nepal are particularly difficult, and the low status of women in this society is one of the driving forces behind girls being trafficked. Associations have started to rise up in support of women's rights and the wall of discrimination has begun to show the first signs of crumbling, but advances in this area are slow.

The problem starts with arranged marriages. Even though the Nepali weddings are colorful and beautiful, and have many interesting traditional aspects, in many cases brides enter into marriage unhappily. Nepali culture permits a man to reject the arranged bride or even to have more than one spouse. In this case, the man is not considered adulterous. But women do not have the same freedom. Any woman who acts this way would face discrimination and tragic outcomes.

In general, the bride is not respected as a human being who has dreams and feelings of her own. Once married, she becomes essentially a servant, her mother-in-law's maid and often a scapegoat. The bride will live with her in-laws in the same house. This ensures that the husband remains under the authority and influence of his parents and the wife has no one to take her side and protect her interests. In Nepal, there is a saying that a good wife is one that gets up early and does all the work for the mother-in-law. All the frustration and humiliation the mother-in-law suffered when she married is now transferred to the daughter-in-law in a vicious cycle of bitterness and hurt. Hurting people hurt people.

If a couple does not have children, the woman is considered cursed, even if it's the husband who is sterile. The absence of children in a marriage gives the husband the cultural right to have sexual relations with other women. In order to obtain even minimal honor, a Nepali woman must be fertile.

Having a male child is valued above all in Nepali society. Not having a male child is believed to create a spiritual void in the family, as well as a practical void, as males are prized for heavy labor and farming and to support the parents in their old age. If no boy is born, once again, it is the woman's fault. In this context, the birth of a girl is seen as a burden. In India as well as Nepal we have heard men say, "I don't care if a girl is born, as long as it is at the neighbor's house." This proverb illustrates how poorly girls are received into the family.

Under Nepali law, a woman only has a right to citizenship if a man—her father or husband—grants it, which seldom happens. People are lobbying to change this policy, but it has yet to change. This makes it extremely difficult for us to get citizenship papers,

ID cards or passports for our girls who are fatherless or whose father has rejected them.

With all these factors at play, it is not surprising that women and girls are sold, abused and devalued.

How Nepali Girls are Trafficked

Girls are not randomly snatched off the street and sold into red light areas. In every case I have seen, someone the girl knew was involved in trafficking her, or the girl herself was deceived and extorted. Some girls are trafficked by their family members or neighbors. Some go to the big cities in search of work and fall prey to traffickers while cut off from their support systems. Some are tricked into false marriages. Some are deceived with the promise of factory or housework that offers a good salary.

In many cases, the girl's closest relatives are involved in the transaction. These same relatives—brothers, cousins and even parents—will be the ones who reject the girl if she attempts to return to the family. The price for a young girl is typically 50,000 to 90,000 Nepalese Rupees ($400–800 USD). This is a small fortune to a struggling family. We have also seen cases where girls were sold for less than $20.

Trafficking does not always involve the movement of people across borders. We've seen plenty of cases where girls were exploited among their own village communities. However, in Nepal, we see that many, many girls and women are trafficked out of the country into India or to the Middle East. The promise of good work and dreams fulfilled in the big cities is hard to pass up. But those dreams quickly turn into nightmares once they cross the border.

Some girls are led to leave home by relatives or community members with the justification that, in the city, they will have better life opportunities. Traffickers attract young people by offering them a good education or the chance to make better money in a respectable job. Many girls, as well as their parents, believe these stories and easily fall prey. I know for a fact that most mothers and fathers would not turn their girls over to the traffickers if they knew the true future that awaited them.

Once they arrive in the city, girls are used as maids without pay. They work many hours each day without adequate food, usually in subhuman conditions. The sexual abuses are numerous and sexual exploitation is just the next step. The newspapers commonly tell stories of Nepali girls used in semi-slave work in India; in restaurants, circuses, hotels and red light areas. They eat poorly, sleep poorly, are physically and sexually abused and, many times, receive no salary. In the majority of cases, the girls say they had no idea they would be participating in this type of life. They were, almost always, deceived. Ignorance is one of, if not the main, weapon of traffickers.

We have had many girls with us who were trafficked by means of false marriages. In this scenario, a young man, who is in reality a trafficker, infiltrates a village. After some days there, he contracts a marriage with a young lady—preferably with a girl who possesses the most attractive physical features. Next, this girl is taken by her "husband" to a major city. Upon arriving in the capital, Kathmandu, or in one of the major cities of India, the girl discovers that her "husband" is actually a trafficker. But by then it is already too late.

Rani married at age 16 and went with her supposed husband to India. Arriving there, she was placed in a hotel while the husband went to work. She soon learned that he had sold her to the hotel for sexual exploitation, and that in three days she would receive her first clients. Rani never saw her husband again. She was given no choice but forced prostitution to pay off her "debt" (the amount paid by the hotel to her husband), in the hopes of someday making her way back home.

By the time girls arrive at the red light areas, they are already in debt. The cost of food, transportation, clothes and everything else is added to their bill, as well as the price that was paid for each of them. If they want to leave, they have to pay their debts in full, an amount that generally grows with each passing day. A trafficked girl's money remains in the possession of the manager or madam, so she can never actually succeed in freeing herself from her debts. The only options are to accept the situation or try to flee. Meanwhile, the threats, the constant vigilance and violence and the police—who are often in bed with the traffickers and pimps—make escaping nearly impossible.

Trafficked girls do not have access to sufficient food. They are forced to service 5–35 clients per day. The average is 14. They suffer physical and psychological torture as well as contracting various diseases linked to sexual violence (few clients use condoms). Men who frequent red light areas do not have much fear of AIDS, nor is it a concern of the managers and madams. Many trafficked girls contract the HIV virus before they are 18 years old. Some die of malnutrition or diseases such as tuberculosis and AIDS, others are killed while trying to escape. Often they die from infection caused by damage to their internal organs.

According to a 2008 report from the Government of India's Ministry of Women and Child Development, 40% of the girls in red light areas in India are minors.[7] The statistics call them minors, but children would be a more appropriate term, as some are under 10 years old.

Many children are indirectly involved in the sex trade because it is their mother's profession. These children grow up in sexually promiscuous and violent environments and are eventually pushed into the same line of work as their mothers. This is all they know—they aren't aware that there are other less harmful options available. They start begging when they are small and by pre-adolescence they are involved in commercial sexual exploitation.

Several girls who have come through our homes were the daughters of women in forced prostitution. These girls were rescued as part of a prevention plan. Most had no desire to go back and visit their mothers—this gives an idea of how traumatic their situation must have been.

Children are much sought after in the trafficking market. They are seen as valuable because of the belief that their virginity can give virility or even cure AIDS. Pre-adolescents or young teen girls, showing the early changes of puberty, are also seen as particularly attractive.

A desirable young girl—or child—will have guaranteed clients waiting for her in the city. Because of this, she is spared from being raped by her traffickers during transport. Arriving at the destination, she is placed in a nice hotel where she is treated well, fed well and kept in a good condition. Then, someone important

---

[7] Ministry of Women and Child Development, Government of India, with assistance from the United Nations Office of Drugs and Crime (UNODC), *India Country Report: To Prevent and Combat Trafficking and Commercial Sexual Exploitation of Children and Women* (New Delhi, 2008), 14.

(from an economic point of view) is contacted.

"A virgin girl is at your disposal," the VIP is told.

Once the business is arranged, the girl is held at the mercy of this client for several days. He is generally an important businessman or someone very financially successful. The price he pays for his time with such a girl is much higher than what was paid for her in her village. The profit for the trafficker is exorbitant. The suffering for the child is unimaginable.

These young girls continue to be a fountain of income for those that exploit them. The younger, fairer-skinned, more beautiful and taller girls bring in a higher profit. With continued use and abuse, a girl's price begins to fall, until it reaches less than a dollar per sexual encounter. By this point, she is considered sick and unproductive.

Nepali girls are especially desired in the trafficking market due to their unique physical features. The co-mingling of the Nepali population with the neighboring countries of China and India has given them physical characteristics that are seen as beautiful and exotic, including lighter skin and an East Asian eye shape. This preference for light skin is a lingering effect of British colonization.

According to a study conducted by the International Labour Organization (ILO) in 2001, an estimated 12,000 Nepali children are trafficked out of the country each year.[8] This number is now considerably outdated, and even at that time likely underestimated the true scope of the problem. Besides India, China

---

[8] International Labour Organization, *Investigating the Worst Forms of Child Labour No. 2: Nepal Trafficking in Girls With Special Reference to Prostitution: A Rapid Assessment* (2001).

and the Middle East are also major destination points for the trafficking of Nepali girls.

In India, the trafficking market brings in millions of dollars *each day*. It is a market that employs thousands of people, not only in forced prostitution, but also in secondary businesses such as restaurants, taxis and hotels. This powerful commerce machine corrupts from the police to high-level government politicians.

Once, in Delhi, I asked my rickshaw driver to take me to the most well known prostitution area in India—G.B. Road. The upper floors of the old buildings were locked with enormous chains on the outside to keep the girls from escaping. I had been in this area some months earlier and seen the precarious conditions girls were forced to live in. This time, I pretended to be a client interested in spending time with a girl. When my rickshaw driver heard this, and also recognized that I was a foreigner, he insisted I not go to that location. Instead, he wanted to take me to a higher-level area.

He tried to persuade me, saying they had better girls in other places. But I knew this location, G.B. Road, held the largest concentration of Nepali girls. I asked him about the price of an encounter with a girl here. He explained to me that a Nepali would cost about three times less than "a good girl from Gujarat" (an Indian state). I stretched the questioning out a little more and asked why a Nepali would be so cheap. His response was emphatic, and distressing to hear: "Nepalis are worthless!"

A girl's arrival at G.B. Road meant she had already spent much time in other red light areas considered higher level. This was the end of the line—the final stage, the lowest level of prostitution in Delhi.

On another occasion I was in Mumbai, the largest city in India and possibly the largest prostitution market in all of Asia. I had left Rose and David in the airport while I walked around trying to find a reasonable hotel where we could spend the night. I met a young man who tried to convince me to stay in a hotel where he would receive a commission for bringing in a client. Without knowing my wife and son waited at the airport, he proposed an encounter with some young girls of 14 and 15 years old. I could choose the nationality from among India's neighboring countries.

In recent years, we have seen Asian governments begin to give timid signs of resistance to child sex trafficking.[9] In Nepal, the media has begun to demand more efficient action against the problem of trafficking. Various local and international organizations have sought to do the good work of restoration, prevention and building public awareness of the issue. Some international governments and media have begun to focus their eyes on this problem and offer suggestions for its prevention as well. We constantly hear of events and seminars focused on combating the trafficking of Nepali girls. These are encouraging signs that something practical is beginning to be done on a larger scale. The subject is being treated with a little more attention, and in a less prejudiced or culturally-biased manner.

---

9 The South Asia Area Counsel of Countries (SAARC) unites Nepal, India, Pakistan, Bangladesh, Sri Lanka, Bhutan and Maldives. SAARC meetings in recent years have broached the problem and tried to create means to slow the advance of child trafficking. In these meetings, preventive and punitive methods have been created.

A major challenge is that the governments need to work in harmony. Nepal and India need to work together to devise efficient action against the problem. When we first started this work, there were few interchanges between these governments. All of the practical work was being done by NGOs (non-governmental organizations, i.e. charities). In 2007, when we began repatriating girls from India, the Nepali government did not have any official mechanisms to aid the process. The border officials were often complicit, or at least inefficient, when dealing with child trafficking, and overcomplicated the rescue work.

The police have arrested some traffickers, but the numbers are pitiful in comparison to the number of girls trafficked. Sometimes, the police themselves have been corrupted by trafficking money. Many times, cases get lost in foolish, bureaucratic details. Sometimes, when cases arrive in supreme court, the court demands more time than the people and witnesses involved can give. Other times, willing witnesses cannot be found. In many cases, girls are hesitant to denounce their traffickers out of fear that the circumstances could turn against them. They also fear discrimination by the police and society, and know the inefficiency of the legal system in punishing the true culprits. With good reason, girls do not trust the mechanisms of the law to support them. Because of all these factors, girls are often reluctant, or even hostile, about seeking legal help.

Although I criticize the action of the police in general, each time we have needed them for a specific matter, we have been helped. The Tourist Police, who specialize in helping foreigners, have been particularly helpful, as have the local Kathmandu police. In recent years we have seen some law enforcement bodies like the CIB (Crime Investigation Bureau) being very efficient in rescues and investigating cases of human-trafficking and child sexual exploitation. We are happy to see these improvements in law enforcement as well as an increase in prosecutions, with more traffickers being put behind bars.

There are several other nonprofit organizations that do good work in the area of child trafficking here, including Maiti Nepal, Shakti Samuha and Tiny Hands. Maiti Nepal has carried out extensive awareness programs in the villages. They, along with other organizations, have teams working on the borders, trying to prevent Nepali girls from being trafficked, and even monitoring police border activity. Over the years, the situation has been slowly improving, but there is still a long way to go.

Chapter 11
Homecoming

In 2007, we sent Mamata to India to further our partnerships with organizations who were repatriating rescued girls to Nepal. Her tales of the trip to Kolkata, Mumbai and Delhi, as well as cities on the India-Nepal border, were devastating. The bureaucratic dynamic between these two countries made the rescue and repatriation process extremely difficult. The complicated laws that made it easy to traffic a girl out of Nepal were the same laws that made it challenging to bring her back into the country.

Shortly after Mamata's trip, we welcomed our first trafficking survivor repatriated from India. She came to us through a shelter called Sanlaap in Kolkata. Gradually, more survivors came to us from India—a couple in 2008 and a few more in 2009. Each time, we would go to the Indian border in Birgunj to pick them up.

It felt like a long time between arriving in Nepal in 2000 and getting our first rescued girl in 2007, but those were important years of learning and building our model for healing. If the rescued girls had come earlier, we might not have been ready. By 2007 we were strong in our idea of family and our model for healing. Most importantly, having our own First Generation girls as leaders in the organization made a huge difference with girls repatriated from India.

By 2010, we had more than 200 kids in care at Apple, across five houses in Kathmandu. Many were prevention cases, rescued from the streets, child labor, domestic violence and extreme poverty. Some had been forced to beg or to sell their bodies to survive. Others were referred to us because they were about to be sold.

One day, a man from International Justice Mission (IJM) came to meet us and see our homes. IJM is a large, reputable organization working at the forefront of trafficking intervention and policy development, so building a relationship with them would be pivotal in furthering our work of caring for repatriated girls. Next, IJM sent Rupa Chetru to visit our homes. She was a Nepali counselor who was working for IJM in India. Soon after, two of their representatives came from Kolkata and we officially entered into a partnership.

Now flocks of girls started flowing to Apple, from IJM and through other channels as well. Girls would arrive at midnight, by bus or by train. The local police would also call us to get girls rescued locally. The first large group of 15 girls arrived through IJM in July of 2010. They had suffered years of horrific violence and nightly rapes in the red light areas of Kolkata, Mumbai and Delhi. Their trauma was higher than the cases we had seen up to that point.

We developed a process for receiving new girls, designed to make them feel immediately valued, safe and cherished. Our welcome parties became an integral part of the healing process. More than just opening our doors, we wanted to help open their hearts. We prepared flower garlands, called mala, and scarves, called katha, which we draped over the girls' shoulders.

Sometimes they tried to take these off, saying, "You don't know who I am, where I am coming from. I don't deserve this."

They didn't feel worthy to have the malas and kathas. We would tell them, "We know who you are and where you come from. We *want* to honor you. You are starting a new time in your life."

We would prepare bags full of gifts and hire a band to play welcoming songs. The following day, we would take the girls to the mall and invite them to choose a teddy bear or any cuddly toy they wanted. We did this to show them that, here, they were free to be kids again. At first, girls would be very hesitant to choose something. They had not been allowed to be children for a long time. They were afraid of everything and everyone. But with the encouragement of other girls who had been at Apple longer, they would eventually get into the spirit, and joyfully select a soft toy to cuddle at night. Girls would cry with joy, and something like relief, when they finally understood that this gift was really for them, that they truly were safe and loved here.

We also received girls rescued from exploitation in Nepal itself. Their cases tended to be very different from those sold to India, and it was actually even harder to help them. The girls rescued from within Nepal generally had a bit more choice in the matter, and they had been earning and keeping some of the money. It was harder for them to see the danger of their situation. The girls who had been trafficked to India didn't want to go there and hadn't even realized what was happening to them. They were forced, sold. They had experienced hell, and when they came here, in their words, they experienced heaven. They took every opportunity. They wanted to go to school. They wanted to recover their dream to be a normal child, and then a normal adult.

Our First Generation girls, and all those rescued under a prevention plan, had their own trauma. They were also hurt, betrayed and neglected. Some had experienced sexual abuse and violence. But the trauma of the girls trafficked to India was even more severe. They came to us in a state of extreme distress. Their sense of unworthiness was even deeper than that of the prevention cases. They felt dirty and undeserving, but when we showed them the truth of their human worth, they were ready to embrace the healing. The love they received here was something they had never experienced before, and it healed them faster than we expected. These survivors wanted to start new, to leave the past behind. They were desperate to heal, so they did. At first we did a lot of listening, and then we adapted our systems to serve them better. We added more formal counseling and our whole team was further trained in trauma-sensitive care.

Anjali

Anjali Tamang (her real name, as she is an anti-trafficking activist who has chosen to speak publicly about her experience) was just 11 when she was trafficked to India by men from her own village in central Nepal. Because she was so small, the traffickers gave her growth hormones to accelerate puberty. A week after starting her period, she was forced to begin taking customers.

After being rescued in 2009 at age 14, Anjali was repatriated to Nepal in July 2010, along with that first large group of 15 girls who came to live at The Apple of God's Eyes. Despite all she had endured, Anjali held on to a beautiful dream: she wanted to go back to her village to open a school and prevent the trafficking of the next generation.

Since the very first day she arrived, we noticed that Anjali was an active person who dreamed, but also pursued her dream with strong and consistent motivation. We were inspired many times when she would speak about her plans to go back to her village and build a school. She told everybody not to judge the people in her village who had sold her. She said they had no knowledge of how badly trafficking could affect children. Even as a young girl, she had these insights and this remarkable ability to forgive, to understand and to keep moving forward.

Nina

Nina came to us in the same group as Anjali. On the plane from the Nepalese border to Kathmandu, one of the people providing security for the group told me about Nina's strength and determination. He told me about her strong way of thinking and doing things properly. So I kept my eyes on her, believing this was a person who would reach her goals.

Time passed and day by day Nina showed more of her potential. One day, Dr. José was visiting with a group from Brazil. We planned a simple ceremony where he could meet some of the girls rescued from India. This would be a hugely meaningful moment, as it was his experience in India all those years ago that sparked the vision which was now providing care and healing for these girls today. It was supposed to be a special time with just Dr. José, myself, Rose and some girls rescued from India. But Rose convinced me to let the whole group join the meeting, as she felt others would be inspired by it. I was quite defensive, because I didn't like to tell people which of our girls had been trafficked and which hadn't. It is very important to us to protect the girls' privacy, and not tell their stories to others. It is up to each person whether she wants to share her story, and with whom. Also, we didn't want to separate the trafficked girls from the prevention cases, or make anyone feel different or self-conscious. But the girls agreed with Rose in this case that we should open the ceremony to everyone.

The girls had prepared a drama to perform. To my surprise, they reenacted the exact scene Dr. José had seen in Mumbai years before (the dead girl on the sidewalk in the red-light area), which had given him the dream for The Apple of God's Eyes. In the drama, one of the girls lay down on the floor as a dead person and others came and lifted her up. That was emotional enough for one evening, but there was more...

Nina thanked Dr. José for envisioning the project, thanked us for bringing it to life and expressed gratitude to everyone involved in her rescue and repatriation. She talked about the suffering of girls trapped in Indian red light areas. As she spoke, she cried out in pain. She told of her desire to work against human trafficking, and the way she spoke was so powerful that even those who had been working in the anti-trafficking field for years understood the pain in a new and very real way. She painted the picture in colors we had never seen before. Her speech affected our team deeply, and many were in tears. Anjali also made a remarkable statement about not just persecuting traffickers in the villages, but providing education and teaching communities how damaged a child could be if she was trafficked. She also talked about forgiving the parents who did this to their children, not just putting them behind bars.

Dr. José was not only crying but literally howling in pain after hearing Nina and Anjali's words. In this moment we came to understand Nina and Anjali's true strength. We could see that both girls had voices as advocates for all those still trapped in the red light areas of India. They told us that they wanted to work to free them all.

That guy on the plane was right. There was a woman of steel behind Nina's gentleness. Nina's quiet manner misled people into thinking she was weak, but behind that sweet face and tiny body was a warrior.

Nina was diagnosed with tuberculosis, which she had contracted in the red light area (where TB is a major problem). She had to get intensive treatments for that illness, but she never gave up her inner strength. She didn't want to hug people because she was afraid they could be infected, but Rose insisted on hugging her, saying she wasn't afraid. What Nina had to "infect" people with wasn't any disease, but a passion to work against injustice.

One day while walking in her village, Nina heard about a girl in the process of being trafficked to India. She went and rescued the girl, and brought her to Apple to be protected. Nina now dreams of becoming a lawyer to defend the rights of children and help free those trapped in red light areas. She wants to fight for traffickers to be prosecuted and properly sentenced for their crimes.

Sarita

Sadly, there have been a few girls who were not able to recover from their past. They simply could not accept that there was a way out for them. No matter how much we talked to them about the good possibilities for their lives, they would voluntarily return to a life of sexual exploitation and begging. This was the case with Saritai. She was trafficked to India and experienced the horror of forced prostitution in Mumbai. According to what she told us, she was finally able to flee and return to Nepal through the help of a Catholic priest.

When we found her, Sarita was living on the streets of Kathmandu, still working in the sex trade. Despite what she had suffered, she was joyful and fun. But she had a serious problem: she had internalized the pattern of abuse. Sex had become an addictive behavior for her, and she was unable to break that pattern. Perhaps this was her attempt to take control of something that had been used against her.

We brought Sarita into the care of our home, but no matter how much we counseled her, she could not seem to control this destructive pattern of behavior. She habitually harassed our male staff, the young men who would deliver food and water, the older boys in our homes and visitors. After almost four months with us, Sarita left our home to get married. But days later she was already separated from the man and back selling her body on the streets. Two years later, Sarita returned to us, now with a baby in her arms. She was seeking shelter again in our house, sorry to have left us. Of course we welcomed her home with open arms.

Restoration of trafficked girls was never easy. The majority of them felt unworthy and inferior, like Sarita. They thought that they were broken, that they had no rights and deserved nothing good in life. Our greatest challenge was getting them to have confidence in themselves. Teaching them to dream again was a daily task.

Pinky

Pinky was a beautiful and kind kid. She came to our home in 2015, around age 18, with a group of girls from Mahima Home in Kolkata, after being rescued from a red light area. One day, shortly after arriving to us, the girls were traveling in the van, driving from one place to another. Pinky became very fearful, saying, "Which brothel are you taking us to now?" They were so used to being circulated.

When girls first come here they are always suspicious. They have been tricked so many times before. Even though they have been told they are being rescued, they don't trust it. Pinky was the first girl in that group to understand that they were safe here, and the first to break down in tears.

Many kids are kind, but Pinky's kindness exceeded others. It takes time for girls to adjust to their new environment and build trust. They are not perfect angels—they are often unhappy, they complain and they are understandably angry. They make enemies. They close their hearts. They fight with each other. They are uncooperative. But Pinky wasn't like that. She never complained, she always followed the rules and never argued. Pinky now works at our school as a nursery teacher. She lives in an apartment on the school grounds and helps keep the school safe.

Anaya

Anaya came with the large group in 2010, along with Anjali and Nina. She was making great progress and slowly healing. Then, in 2012, we got a call from Marcia saying that five armed police had come to Home 1 to arrest Mamata. But Mamata was currently out of the country. According to the police, she had illegal custody of a girl whose mother wanted to take her back! When we saw the details of the case, we realized the girl was Anaya.

We produced the paperwork to prove that we did indeed have legal custody. The police confirmed that everything was legal and in order, and left. But the next day they came back, and we had to go with them to the station to prove once again that this accusation was false.

At the police station there was one Indian lawyer, one Nepali lawyer and a police inspector. Our own lawyer was away in the United States at the time, so Eliza (one of the home leaders from our First Generation), who was in her sixth month of law school, had to defend the case. Next, the Human Rights Commission summoned Marcia and threatened her. I went to their office wearing a suit (unusual for me), and said, "You guys are supposed to protect human rights, but instead you are on the side of the traffickers!"

They responded, "We were told that you stole this girl from her mother and have illegal custody."

"That is absolutely false," I said. "All the papers are here. Read the case! This Indian lawyer, Mr. Prabin, who you think is a lawyer, is himself a trafficker, mentioned here in the newspaper."

"But he gave us his business card from the Human Rights Commission of Mumbai," they argued.

I pushed back, "Call the Human Rights Commission of Mumbai and ask if that person works there." So she did, and of course no one by that name was employed there. He had just given them a business card that anyone could print on any street corner.

Eliza defended the case very well, two times. Anaya's mother came into court crying and saying, "I miss my daughter."

We responded with what Anaya had told us: "You are a brothel owner. You put your daughter to work in that place. You put her sister to work there also, and then you sold her to another brothel."

The mother continued to deny this, saying, "No, that is not true. I work in a restaurant in Kolkata. I have no brothel."

As the case went on, our lawyer came back from the US.

Normally, he preferred to make deals and agreements rather than cause a big fight. But on the day he defended us in court he was so bold—he was like a lion. He spoke strongly, saying, "Mr. Prabin, I am going to put you in jail. You are not a lawyer. You are pretending to be a lawyer." I was amazed by his boldness.

Afterwards, he told me that when he had been driving to Apple, he got stuck in a traffic jam. While stopped, he noticed a well dressed guy in a shop buying a single cigarette. A lady was with him, and she refused to buy him another one. Why would a well dressed guy, with an expensive suitcase, only be able to buy one cigarette? Our lawyer then recognized that this guy was Mr. Prabin, and immediately understood that he was just a trafficker disguised as a lawyer in a fancy suit.

Anaya herself testified about everything, against her own mother. I can't imagine how difficult this must have been for her. In the end, we won the case. We told Anaya's mother and the guy pretending to be a lawyer, "You leave this child alone or we will put you in jail!"

They left and we never heard from them again. At Anaya's request, we didn't push to get her mother thrown in jail. She didn't want to go with her mother, but she didn't want her put in jail either.

As our homes grew, we worked increasingly to disrupt the flow of child trafficking to India. We continued to learn about the issue, as it was constantly changing. We built connections with more people working within India, and also in the Nepali government. Mamata began leading teams to India regularly to establish contacts in the red light areas of Kolkata, Delhi and Mumbai.

This work has never been easy, mainly because most people are afraid to get involved. Some people have preconceived notions about trafficked girls and blame the victims, and others use bureaucratic and political problems as an excuse for not taking action. Many people become exhausted from the trauma, stress and overall difficulty of commitment needed to walk alongside children in their recovery. And, as Anaya's story shows, there is no small risk of retaliation from traffickers when working with girls still trapped in exploitation, or those recently rescued.

Chapter 12
The Earthquake

Nepal is a very high risk area for earthquakes. The Himalayas actually grow a little bit each year because of how much the tectonic plates are moving underground. Over the years we had experienced several minor earthquakes—one in 2001 caused houses to move a few centimeters from the sidewalk, but it was still very light.

In 2013 our team went through some earthquake training: how to react, how to prepare a stock of medicine and water and how to always have an emergency bag ready to go. Many people thought the training was useless—nobody really believed a big earthquake would come. Nonetheless, we bought earthquake alarms and installed them in all our homes.

According to the news, Nepal gets a major earthquake around every 70 years. The last big one, an 8.0, had been in 1934 and killed more than 10,000 people. If this "rule" of 70 years was true, then the next earthquake was 11 years late.

In early April of 2015 I had a nightmare of many buildings collapsing. I woke up quite shaken and wondered if I should tell anyone about the terrible dream. I was worried people might think I was being paranoid, so I was reluctant to share it. But I decided to tell my team anyway, saying "Guys, maybe that was only a bad dream, but let's check the earthquake alarms all the same. Make sure they are tuned up and have charged batteries." Thankfully, some people took me seriously and checked the alarms.

Then, on April 25th, 2015, the nightmare became reality.

Everything looked normal that morning. We had a beautiful breakfast at home with some friends who were visiting. Then we all split up and went to different places. I took one of our friends to a church quite close to my house, around a 12 minute drive. The church was built on the very edge of a mountain.

The sound system in the building was very loud, but even with all the noise, I could hear a sound like a small explosion. Through my feet I felt something like small electrical waves. After a few seconds I realized that yes, the ground was indeed moving. I rushed out of the church building and saw everything shaking sideways and up and down. In one area, part of the mountain was falling down and I narrowly escaped being crushed.

That tremor lasted only 45 seconds (we later learned), but it felt like hours. Once the shaking stopped, I realized that this was a major earthquake. I began to think about the state of my family. Terrible thoughts took over my mind, like, "Will my wife still be alive? Did my children survive?"

As I rushed to the front of the church looking for my shoes, I noticed that my socks were cold and wet—a water tank had fallen off the building terrace and broken. Even today, whenever I remember that moment I still feel my feet wet from that water.

Thankfully, I found the friend who had come with me and we went home as quickly as possible. I was very afraid for my family and for all our kids.

THE EARTHQUAKE

On the way, I got news from Mamata saying Asha was safe and unharmed. Then, my phone rang again and it was my son David, saying he was fine, and asking about me, Rose and Asha. I told him the news about Asha but I didn't have any updates from Rose. In that moment, I was torn between relief that David and Asha were fine, and terrible worry for Rose. I kept calling her but the call wouldn't go through, and when it finally did go through, there was no answer.

I drove frantically towards home. As we got closer, it gave me hope to see that the buildings on the way hadn't collapsed. At the gate of our complex I saw, with immense relief, Rose rushing towards me. I told her our children were alive and well.

Reflecting back on that day, Rose shared,

> The earthquake was our worst experience in Nepal. For years I was scared because geologists were saying Nepal's earthquake would be above 11. When I actually started to feel it, and it didn't stop like all the times before, I was sure I was dead. My heart and my soul were overcome with fear. It's unexplainable. It was like the ground was waves. Silvio was in one place, David in another, Asha in another, and me at home. I had no hope of us all surviving…I just thought, "When will I die? How can we possibly protect so many kids? How can we be safe?"
>
> When you are human, the safest place is the land, the earth. And when you lose that, you lose everything, because you do not feel secure. Before the big earthquake, I was very courageous, even fearless. But after that, I lost my confidence. When we lose the place where we stand, it's so hard. Sometimes people think we are superheroes, that we have no fear. But we are human like

everyone. We have fear like everyone. We just choose to trust in God. And to keep going.

After a few more minutes we got in contact with Asha by phone. She was calm in the care of Grandpa Lucas. All the Apple kids were also fine, thank God. We gathered with our neighbors in an open area, and soon learned from the news that this had been a 7.8 magnitude earthquake, with hundreds of deaths already counted in the first hour.

David finally made his way back to us after navigating roads blocked by debris. He had been driving when the earthquake hit, and could feel his car shaking from side to side. Once the earthquake stopped he quickly drove ahead towards home. On the way, he saw other cars completely destroyed by debris, with dead bodies inside. A few hours later we met up with Lucas and Asha—I cannot describe the relief I felt to have her back in our arms.

We spent a while playing taxi to our staff and children who needed help getting back home from wherever they had been when the earthquake hit. Many of the roads were too damaged to drive on, so our buses and vans could not get very far. We loaded kids in the back of our pickup truck, making several trips to get everyone safely home. Meanwhile, the ground kept shaking with many aftershocks, each one causing more panic for both the children and the adults.

The city was hit hard. There were injured people and dead bodies on the streets. Electrical wires and poles had fallen down and many buildings had completely collapsed. It was apocalyptic.

That night, David and I went out to transport some friends. The city was dark and scary to travel through. The fear of

THE EARTHQUAKE

aftershocks was all too real. As we drove by the biggest hospital in Nepal, we saw a sea of people looking for their relatives and friends, many of whom were surely already gone.

That first night the death toll was already more than 1,400 and growing by the minute. The situation was much were worse than we thought at the beginning. We slept inside our cars that first dark night.

The next day, our team mobilized like I had never seen before. With how damaged the roads were, we predicted that Kathmandu's food supply might be hit hard and cause a rush on the stores. So the young leaders went to buy food first thing that morning. After a few hours some of the leaders told me, "Uncle, we already have food for one week." After a few more hours they told me, "We have food for one month."

We decided to move everyone to our school for safety, to make logistics easier and to keep an eye on all our kids in one central place. Members of the community living around our school had asked to use one of the sports courts, so when we got there with all the kids, there were already over 200 people at our small school. The kids from Apple took over another sports court, so now there were over 300 people at the second sports court, made up of the kids from our homes, some relatives, our staff and our foreign guests.

In the beginning, the atmosphere was tense with hundreds of us all crammed into a small property. Everyone was looking for the best spot. Some volatile conversations took place between families from the community. We offered to share our food, and they declined at first, but eventually came to eat with us. On that first night sleeping at the school it began to rain, and even more people came to seek shelter there. At that moment, between the two sports courts, more than 500 people were sheltered.

We were sleeping outside with hundreds of kids in makeshift tents, all very improvised. There were many aftershocks, which further traumatized the children, and people were quick to panic. It was, understandably, hard to keep calm in this environment. I brought the guitar from my home and gave it to Saili. I thought her singing might ease the children's anxiety. As I was out running an errand, I remembered that many neighbors were also sheltering alongside us and instantly worried the music would disturb them, as everyone was still tense. But when I got back to the school, I saw Saili singing with the kids, with the neighbors watching and even singing along. Saili told me that she had tried to end the music hours before, but every time she stopped, the neighbors would ask her to keep singing. They said her music was like "opening the skies and keeping the darkness away." On the second day, the neighbors brought a whole goat to share with us.

One of the hardest moments was when—without consulting others, as I usually did with important decisions—I made the choice to send any Brazilian staff and visitors who had kids back to Brazil. That decision hit many people hard. In some moments I thought maybe I was overreacting, because surely the worst moments had passed. But my decision was soon proven to be the correct one. On May 12th, a second earthquake hit Nepal. The second earthquake was weaker than the first one, but still a 7.3, causing hundreds more deaths. All together both earthquakes led to more than 9,000 reported deaths. In the month that followed, there were a reported 459 aftershocks.

Unfortunately, we saw some people taking opportunities to raise money in the name of "earthquake relief" to benefit themselves. Even some charities did that. The earthquake was a great excuse for people to raise funds "towards earthquake victims in Nepal," but not all donations really reached the victims. Some people used part of the funds to help and then soon left. Some people helped many but also promoted themselves. But there were also many people and organizations who did work honestly and with full commitment.[10]

I saw a lot of things in those days and experienced some of the most profound moments of my life. There were impressive things done by people who live here in Nepal and work with us (some Nepali and some Brazilian), by guests who were visiting and got caught here after the earthquake, and by people who flew in after the earthquake to be of service.

I saw Jorge staying up all night watching for any sign of shaking so he could ring a bell and alert everyone to rush to a safe place. Augusto, Graziele and others also helped, taking turns so that somebody would always be awake if aftershocks came. I saw Graziele walking through sleeping kids and pulling blankets over them, as kids would kick them off or have them taken by a sleeping neighbor. I saw Marcelo cleaning and unblocking the toilets. This was a huge job, since more than 500 people were using our bathrooms day and night, when they were only intended for part time use by 200 people. I had planned to take on that job myself, but I was truly dreading it. But without saying a word, Marcelo took it upon himself, asking for no thanks or recognition.

---

[10] All funds received by The Apple of God's Eyes/Nepalese Home for earthquake relief were strictly used for earthquake victims and reconstruction. The organization itself contributed more than $25,000 USD to complete the earthquake fund, and no profit was kept for the organization's other programs.

I saw Hari, Deepak, Asish, Bigyan and Bikash going out and risking their lives to check if Asha's blood relatives were alive or not, taking medicine to that faraway village. I saw Marcia and Izabela asking if they could take food to victims in the earthquake epicenter area, sharing and thinking of others when food was so scarce in Kathmandu. I saw David making tents for sick people in our makeshift camp, raising the spirits of everyone,

I saw Rose hugging people as a mother, to calm their hearts when she herself was uneasy, cooking food for others, and always keeping an eye out for anyone who was cold, sick or distressed. I saw Rute jumping in to relieve Rose and others from any burden of cooking. I saw Bikash finding a way to buy tarpaulins when they were incredibly hard to find. I saw Mamata managing many things and giving away money for medicine, food, tents, tarps, etc. as people worldwide started to donate toward Nepal. I saw Eliza Magar, a petite nurse turned into a giant, giving medical aid alongside Dr. Augusto, another giant who helped many people with health issues. I saw Angela, Binda, Joshuda and many others taking care of people and bringing them comfort.

I saw Lucas going by motorbike to the villages, checking the state of local families, some we knew and many we didn't. Often he returned with the report that they were hungry and needing food because they had lost everything. I saw Shova comforting traumatized children, and leading a canteen team to keep everyone fed. I saw Saili and Sandip singing with their full hearts, bringing people out of their panic. Many times people were brought to tears by their music. People were praying for the land to become stable. One of the most profound scenes I witnessed was Urmila—one of the kids living at Apple—praying with a Nepalese flag, asking God to help her nation..

THE EARTHQUAKE

During those days I saw Nepalese people crying in a way I had never seen before, which opened my heart to love these people even more. Many times I had heard people say that the Nepalese weren't emotional, but here I saw people weeping hard from desperation and lack of hope. I wanted to hug them, saying simply, "There is hope." I hugged many. I looked into the eyes of many. I wanted to somehow express to them, "We care, we are together in this crisis." We grew closer to many people from the community. Normally, before the earthquake, we would just say "Hello," and sometimes even that wasn't said.

The loss was catastrophic and unfathomable. The whole country was hurt and bleeding. In some places, like Sindulpalchowk, we could smell the bad odor of bodies decomposing under the rubble. We saw many bodies being burnt on the pyres of cremation spread around the Bagmati River (this is the customary Hindu funeral practice). We saw trucks heaped with bodies to be cremated. I saw an article about a man who lit funeral pyres four times in one week. The last was for his daughter. I also saw a lot of heroic actions on TV, like a baby being taken alive from the rubble and everyone celebrating.

The world had eyes on Nepal for a change, because of this tragedy. Teams came from Brazil, America, Canada, Japan and many other countries to provide medical care and build shelters for all the people whose homes had been destroyed. Our staff and older girls went along with relief teams to translate and distribute food and water.

Many times I had to hide myself to cry alone when I didn't know what to do. Just a few months earlier I had sought help for panic attacks, but now I was amidst the biggest crisis of my life, and I needed to stay calm to manage the situation for our kids.

Things seemed much bigger than I could handle, but always God found a way to lift me up and guide me. Sometimes a message of encouragement came through the words of a child, a gesture from a friend, help from a stranger or an encouraging phone call from abroad. Somehow I always found the strength to carry on, even in the shadow of the valley of death.

The aftershocks kept coming for another year and a half. During that time it became very difficult to get fuel. There was also a blockade for several months at the Indian border, which prevented supplies from getting through and caused food shortages. There were power outages for 10–12 hours a day. At times the situation became so desperate that we had to go into the forests to gather wood for cooking our food.

Many of our kids and staff were traumatized by the earthquakes, Rose and myself included. There was a large influx of new kids who had been injured in the earthquakes, who had lost parents, or whose homes and even villages had been destroyed. Girls who were already vulnerable became even more vulnerable, and the care that we could offer was needed more now than ever before.

Out of this cold, dark and difficult few years came some great blessings. Hope Force International came in 2016 with a team of American and Canadian engineers and construction experts to build houses for people whose homes had been destroyed. I asked them—and they kindly agreed—to also build some simple, sturdy "earthquake houses" for our leadership team. By that point, our First Generation leaders had been working for the organization for a decade or more. They earned a reasonable

THE EARTHQUAKE

salary but it wasn't enough for them to purchase their own homes, and of course they had no relatives to back them up. I loved the idea of giving them a more secure future through home ownership, and Hope Force made it possible for Marcia, Saili, Mamata and 30 others, including some of our girls who had gone back to live with their relatives in the villages.

A man named Randy Watson also came in that time as an answer to our prayers. Our organization, and the needs we were addressing, had kept growing over the years, but we weren't getting enough funding to cover everything. When the Brazilian economy fell into a crisis, it became difficult for MCM and other key supporters from Brazil to meet their funding commitments. We hoped and prayed for others to come and help.

In the beginning, most of our funding came from MCM in Brazil, and then, over the years, more wonderful people and organizations joined to help us. But even with all these loyal supporters, funding remained our biggest challenge, and the earthquake made things that much more difficult.

Randy was a part of the team that came with Hope Force. I had noticed Randy, but I didn't really get to know him. He was a quiet, self-contained guy, not seeking attention. When he got home, he emailed to say, "I was so impacted by your work. I want to help. Should I raise funds? What can I do for you?"

People often come with big promises, saying, "I'm gonna solve your financial problems." In the early days we used to get so hopeful and happy every time we heard that—and it happened many times. But the promises were almost never kept, so we learned to be skeptical. But after Randy emailed me, he immediately talked to a man named Rob, who then started helping us by supporting our school. Then came Atlas Free, also connected to us by Randy. In 2017, even more generous supporters came, all sent by Randy. He kept asking, "What do you need? I want to relieve your burden." Each time he came to visit Nepal, he would bring new people to see the work and encourage them to donate.

Then, he did something that I am still amazed by today. He decided to leave his very successful construction company and start a Canadian charity called Ally Global Foundation. Randy explained: "Out of all the international work I've seen over the past decade, *this* is the most impactful I've come across. The way leaders are being developed, how invested the national people are, the remarkable outcomes you're seeing in restoration.... I feel called to establish an organization in Canada to come alongside you." He said all this as if it was no big thing.

When one of our graduated girls, now a safe home leader, felt compelled to use her story to help other girls like her, Randy found a way to make it happen. In 2019 he brought a team to Nepal to create a short film with our girls—*The Twelve Thousand*—to raise awareness and money. During this time Randy asked us, "How much is your deficit?" It was $12,000 a month at that point. He said, "Done. Starting next month, we will be sending you that amount."

Randy's support was so much more than money. He became our friend, our brother. He has a gentle spirit and people trust him. He relates to the girls with the utmost dignity and respect. He found a family here, and he and his team relieved our financial burden.

Then, together, we got a bigger vision. We dreamed about purchasing land and building a campus where all five of our homes and our school could be on one property, along with staff housing, a soccer field (critically important!) and a health clinic

THE EARTHQUAKE

and counseling center to serve our kids and the local community. This would relieve the monthly cost of rent and give us room to grow and care for many more kids for decades to come.

As I write this, we have bought the land and construction will begin any day now.[11] Randy and his team plan everything so professionally, working with architects, engineers and Nepali leadership to make sure everything is done with great care and intention. They are teaching us, but also we are teaching them. We are walking in miracles together.

---

[11] Canadian government regulations wanted Ally to buy the land in their name and lease it to Nepalese Home for 99 years. But both our team and Randy's team agreed this wouldn't be empowering. We felt strongly that the land should belong to our local organization, Nepalese Home, so that this legacy can continue long in the future.

Aftermath of the earthquake; April, 2015.

Sheltering at the school after the earthquake; April, 2015.

Chapter 13
The Dream Continues

Over many years, and through the privilege of working with many kids, I have learned a lot about dignity: the circumstances that damage it and the elements needed to recover it. Dignity is absolutely critical for a person's wellbeing. In order to live a meaningful, happy life, you have to feel worthy. When they first came to us, girls would say, "I'm worthless, I'm the garbage of the garbage." Today, we see those same girls—who believed they were no better than the garbage in which they slept and scrounged food from—leading, working, studying and building their own lovely families.

There are many things that can steal a person's dignity. It can evaporate when someone is sick or unable to care for their body and hygiene, or when a person is poor to the point of hunger and homelessness. It can be shattered when someone is evicted from their home. Drug and alcohol dependency, involvement in crime and not having access to education are other situations that can steal dignity. And, as we are most familiar with, dignity can be absolutely destroyed when an individual is sold, exploited and abused with no hope of freedom. No matter how someone's dignity was stolen, these individuals need support and resources to heal and get it back.

There are several stages of rebuilding dignity. In the first stage, we address the immediate need. If someone is hungry on the sidewalk, we provide them with food. The person will feel relieved and, for some time, will no longer feel undignified by their hunger. But hunger will come again; it's a cyclic thing. So dignity needs to be created in a sustainable way. Giving a plate of food is a necessary emergency step but, in the long run, the hungry person needs something more sustainable, a means for feeding themself.

For kids coming out of human trafficking, we first need to give them a safe place to heal. We need to give them a clean bed, not for work, but just for rest. We need to give clothes, medical care and education. These things will help them *begin* the healing process, but after that, step-by-step, they need to keep improving and moving forward.

The second stage of restoring dignity is when the person becomes more actively involved in the process of their healing. In the third stage, they start to have partial responsibility for their expenses and independence. In the fourth stage, the person is fully independent, with their own job or business, education, family and decisions. At this point, the person's dignity has reached the highest level. They are not just helping themself and standing on their own feet, they are also able to help others. It is the greatest gift of my life to see many girls and boys now enjoying that high level of dignity and being of service to others.

I believe that some very simple things have a direct connection to human dignity, such as a bed, shoes and a table. If someone sleeps on the ground to have fun, like camping or sleeping on a beach, that is one thing, but if they have to sleep on the floor because they have no bed, that wounds their dignity. In the red light areas of India, women sleep on mats on the floor. The beds are just "to work." So when a kid comes to The Apple of God's Eyes and gets a bed of her own, just to rest, it gives her a deep sense of worth. Girls get emotional just knowing that their bed belongs to them.

It's the same with shoes. Walking barefoot on the beach because you want to feel the sand is one thing, but walking barefoot because you have no shoes, often experiencing pain and risking cuts and infection—that is another thing. The simple ownership of a nice pair of shoes can be a great source of dignity. Remember my story of how much shoe polish our girls used to go through? Because of this, in our prevention scholarship program, we always give shoes to the kids, as we believe shoes have a direct connection to self-worth.[12]

We can see a similar connection with a table. A dining table symbolizes the gathering of family or friends. Tables are meant to have food on them. For a hungry person, to have food is good, but to have a table with food on it is even better, and brings a feeling of honor. When loved ones eat together at a table, there is even more honor.

But all these things are only the first stage of restoring dignity. In order for a person to truly progress in their healing, they have

---

[12] Time and time again, we see that children who are in school are less vulnerable to trafficking. Because of this, we operate a prevention program where our team identifies high risk villages and supports the children in these communities with scholarships to attend school. To date, we have provided financial support for tuition, school supplies and trafficking awareness to more than 12,000 children living with their families in rural areas of Nepal.

to start believing they are worthy of it. We can provide items like a bed and shoes, and offer the love and support of a family environment, but we cannot force girls to accept dignity.

Sunni

One of the saddest stories I ever encountered was in 2021, during COVID-19. The police called Eliza at 10 p.m. They had just rescued Sunni, age 16, from a red light area here in Kathmandu. She was first arrested, then placed with us at Apple. When she got to Home 1 that same night she told Eliza, "I need to go back to work tomorrow." Eliza told her, "You can't go. You are now under our custody."

Sunni kept insisting, "No, I must go because my sister is sick. I am paying for her treatment." We didn't believe this, because girls who are being sexually exploited in Kathmandu often come up with interesting stories and elaborate reasons why they need to go back to the streets. But after three days Sunni still stuck with her story. She continued insisting that she needed to go. I suggested that Eliza ask Sunni what hospital her sister was in. "Ask for her sister's bed number, get the details," I advised. If it was a story, as we suspected, Sunni would not be able to give these details. But when Eliza asked, Sunni told her right away.

Eliza went to the hospital and learned that the story was true. The girls' father was sleeping under the bed. It was a public hospital and very under-resourced. The father was supposed to administer his daughter's medicine (this is normal in government hospitals), but the nurse said he was always drunk. She also mentioned that the family couldn't afford the medicine. They suspected that the girl had severe tuberculosis. When Eliza asked how soon they would have the diagnosis, the hospital staff explained that the girl was in line to get more tests but it would take another 20 days or so. She had already been waiting more than two months.

Eliza immediately brought the girl, who was 14, to a private clinic to get all the blood tests and diagnostics. Two days later we got the news that it was a metastasized cancer, already spread all over her organs. The doctor told Eliza that the child had just a few days to live. The father wanted to take her home. We offered to take both girls into our home, but the father said, "No, I want to take her home and make her food, and let her die with all her loved ones around her."

We were in a dilemma. Should we let Sunni leave our home to be with her sister? This child had been charged into our care by the police, and the government could be strict about custodial responsibility. Not to mention that Sunni would probably go back into prostitution if released.

Our leadership team had a meeting and decided it was more humane to let Sunni go and stay with her sister. When Eliza came at 5 a.m. to take Sunni to her father's home, the call came,very sadly, that the little sister had already died. Instead of taking Sunni to be with her sister, we took her to the funeral.

We were devastated, but took comfort from the fact that at least the little sister got proper medical attention during the last days of her life. She got to die with dignity. While they were waiting at the hospital, the father told Eliza, "I don't know what my other daughter is doing. I suspect it is something illegal because once I had to go to the police station to get her released. They didn't tell me why, but then she was again arrested and sent to you guys. Always she has money. I'm afraid my daughter is in prostitution."

We never told him the real story. He was already in so much pain. The father was drinking because he was hurting. His baby was dying and he was a loving father. This story really hit my heart. Sunni was selling her body to save her sister.

After her sister died, Sunni came back and stayed with us a few more weeks. Then she wanted to go, so we let her go. Sometimes she still calls our staff and asks for prayers and support. She still feels connected to us.

Grace

Grace was very sick when she came to us. She had been trafficked to Kolkata, where she developed some kind of autoimmune disease. She was so sick that even her trafficker was advising her to leave the red light area. But the other girls always persuaded her to stay, telling her that she would have no place in Nepalese society anymore. They would tell her, "You won't have a place to sit at any table."

However, as Grace's disease got worse, she decided to come back to Nepal. We had launched a program in Kolkata for young women who were thinking of leaving the red light area. This program was not only for young girls but also for older women who had been trafficked for sex when they were teenagers.[13] At 27 years old, Grace was the first woman to come through that outreach program.

---

[13] When trafficked girls become older women, less desirable to clients, often they are no longer kept under lock and key. At that point, it is poverty, stigma, shame, internalized oppression and a lack of alternatives that keeps them trapped in exploitation. Often the only option they were left with was to return to their villages and convince younger relatives to work for them in the same profession.

When Grace arrived, we of course didn't know about the comments she had heard about there being "no place at the table" for her. Shova (one of our housemothers and a First Generation leader) organized a big table with many people sitting together. She then placed Grace at the head of the table, the most honorable seat. Grace was amazed. She saw that those ladies in Kolkata had been wrong. There *was* a place for her.

She committed herself to stay at Apple, and went on to help her sister and other family members escape. Now, Grace is working at our office in India, doing outreach to help Nepali women and children return home. When Rose asked her how she became so committed to this work, she said, "I met God at the table." She was referring to the moment when she was placed in the seat of honor at Shova's table.

Priya

Recently, we got a call about some kids who were about to be trafficked. The mother had run away and the father had been in jail. He was now out of jail, and telling people that he planned to sell his two oldest girls (aged five and seven) to India, and that if he couldn't sell the youngest one (age three), he would drown her in the river.

People told the police, and our field worker in that area, Priya, found out about it. The father was accused and the kids were allowed to come to us. Priya had grown up at Apple and now lives in Nuwakot, where she works as a school teacher. We continue to support her, and she assists us by finding kids who are at risk and sending them to Apple before they can be sold to India.

Jenny

We often have several moms living in our homes with their kids. Some of these families were rescued together from red light areas in India. When Jenny was 11 years old, she got pregnant in her village. She had been selling her body, not for noodles, but just for the *spice packet* that came with the noodles. She was that hungry, that desperate. In exchange for those spices, she had to have sex with older men. One day, she got pregnant. She first went to another shelter home and gave birth there. Then, she ran away, jumping the five meter wall while holding her baby. Thankfully they both survived, but she was caught by the police. They decided to send her to us, rather than back to that first home, because we could provide more psychological support for kids like her.

When Jenny came, nursing her little baby, she was so childish. She was just 12 years old. The housemothers would call her, saying, "Jenny, you need to feed your baby."

Jenny would respond, "Feed him yourself. You also have breasts." She was so naive that she thought any woman could feed her child.

Members of our team took over the care of the baby. We considered sending him for adoption, but Rose suggested we give it one year. If Jenny gained an attachment in one year, the baby could stay. If not, we would recommend adoption. We started sending Jenny to the market to buy food and clothes for the baby, giving her the chance to develop some attachment. We also gave her a lot of space just to be a child herself and to be free of the burden of caring for a baby.

In Jenny's case, she did end up getting attached to her child. But in many other cases, very young mothers, or mothers who got pregnant as a result of rape, would transfer responsibility for the baby to our staff.

Today, Jenny and her son are both excelling under the care of our team. Both of them have even attended our school at the same time. I am so proud of Jenny.

We want kids to be reunited with their family whenever possible. But it is often the case that parents don't accept their kids back. Many mothers would give their lives for their child, but also many mothers are knocking at our gate, asking us to take their kids. In some cases, we would try for years to establish communication and connection with a child's mother, but the mother simply would not come. One mother took seven years to visit her daughter.

Some mothers want to remarry, but don't want to bring their children into the new marriage (because of the caste system, both the child and mother would face shame and discrimination). They will often seek to discard the child, but they also have some love for them and want them to be cared for, so they try to give them to us.

When poverty is the main motivation for giving up their child, we will sometimes offer financial support to help parents keep families together.

Hannah

Hannah had a difficult relationship with her mother. She had always asked Hannah and her sisters for money from their earnings while they were being exploited in India. Then, when Hannah testified in court against her traffickers, the neighbors became hostile to her mother. In the area where Hannah comes from, almost every household has daughters or sisters or a mother in the red light areas of India, or family members who are involved in trafficking. In that community the traffickers are powerful people, and Hannah testifying was a threat to their business.

We built a house for Hannah here in Kathmandu (one of the ones built by Hope Force after the earthquake). Hannah eventually forgave her mother and gave the house to her. Now the whole family is living there.

Dexa
Dexa is a young lady in our home who had been trafficked to India. One of her sisters is still being exploited there. Dexa had been with us four years when she heard that her three little sisters were about to be trafficked as well—her mother was about to sell them. The youngest was only five. Dexa went to the village herself and brought them to safety. They walked all night, through the mountains, arriving at Home 5 in the early morning.

These recent cases are a sharp reminder that there is still much work to do here in Nepal.

At the same time, day by day, more of our kids' dreams are coming true. Our First Generation leaders are running the project with incredible skill and heart. Young women and men who have grown up in our homes are doctors, dentists, nurses, pharmacists, business people, chefs, teachers, social workers, lawyers, engineers and loving parents. Our kids are building a better world in so many different ways.

THE DREAM CONTINUES

Anjali (whose story I shared earlier) has fulfilled her dream of opening a school in her village to prevent the trafficking of girls. She graduated from our school, studied education in college, got a bachelor's degree, raised money (many of our friends and supporters kindly jumped in to help), built a school and opened it in 2021. She is now serving more than 150 children with education and gradually changing the mindset of her community.[14]

As we continue to grow and have beautiful new opportunities, we never want to be seen as a shelter or an institution. We never liked those labels. We are a family; a large family of girls and boys, women and men, who smile, sing, make music, love a pure hug, eat pizza, laugh and play together, cry together sometimes, get really intense about soccer—all the joyful things that sweeten the soul.

Our girls dreamed about going to Brazil in those early days. A few of them later got Brazilian citizenship and went there to stay. Others have emigrated to Australia, Dubai, America and Europe, where they were able to pursue higher education and find good jobs. It seems like every week another young person's dream comes true.

We have set up The Apple of God's Eyes homes in Cambodia, Thailand and Bangladesh. We hope in the future to reach other nations, such as Romania. There is much work to be done, but we are not alone. Many people are doing excellent work in many countries. The girls we have raised, and the girls we will reach in the future, will grow up to reach thousands more, and gradually, this society will change for the better.

---

[14] Anjali tells her own story in her book entitled *Standing in the Way: From Trafficking Victim to Human Rights Activist*, available on Amazon.

The work of healing and restoring dignity is a slow process. It requires time and commitment from the person who is healing, but it also requires time and commitment from individuals who are willing to stand by their side for many, many years. Girls spend an average of 10 years living in the home with us. When you think about it that way, The Apple of God's Eyes is still very young as an organization. But we have seen hundreds of stories of transformation pass through our homes.

The difficulties we have faced over the past 23 years have been many: logistical, financial, emotional, spiritual and cultural. We have faced criticism from people who did not understand our goals or value our approach. But through it all, the wonderful and miraculous experiences sustained and enriched us. The frustrating and painful experiences forced us to grow, and shaped us. The joy has been so much greater than the pain. Hope conquered frustrations. Faith conquered doubt. Love conquered fear.

And now, the girls of the world are counting on you. Those who have not yet been reached are crying out, waiting for someone to see their suffering and help. Those who have been rescued are looking for a seat at the table and a bed to call their own. They await a new tomorrow, a new dream, a new family, a new home, a new hope. I invite you to join us, with whatever is in your hands to give. Let's work together to fulfill that hope!

Receiving new shoes; 2010.

Grace, on her way to India; 2023.

Anjali's school; 2022.

Epilogue

Today, here is what our First Generation girls are up to:

Raquel is a nurse in England. Promila is a doctor. Eliza, Marcia, Gleiva, Isabella and several others are on the leadership team of The Apple of God's Eyes/Nepalese Home. Shova and Joshuda are housemothers raising the next generation of kids in our homes with incredible dedication and love. They have set the standard of care high for other Nepali social workers.

Angela is about to be the owner of a coffee shop. Maili is opening a bakery. Jane is a counselor, providing mental health services to our kids and kids from the community. Selma is the financial director of Nepalese Home; she has a huge amount of responsibility and she handles everything with the greatest care and integrity.

Marcia is married and has a happy life with her husband, Bikash, who also grew up in our homes and is on the leadership team. She has been dreaming of becoming a mother soon. I always tell her she has been a mother for a long time already—she helped raise her own brother and sisters as a young child herself.

Mamata graduated with a Master's Degree in Education and Leadership (M.Ed) from Kathmandu University. She became the principal of our school and plays many other crucial roles at Apple/Nepalese Home. I would often tell her, "Every brick used to build The Apple of God's Eyes has crossed your hands," because, since 2001, she has been instrumental in many areas.

I changed some of the names mentioned in the book to protect the girls' privacy, but some of them gave me permission to use their real names. They want their stories to encourage others that it is possible to overcome the harshest of backgrounds and build a joyful, meaningful life.

These girls used to think they were the ones who got blessed, but their life stories—their struggles, their fight and their perseverance—have blessed *us* more than they could ever imagine.

In 2023, Asha's grandmother came from the village to live with us at our home in Kathmandu. It is our joy and privilege to care for her in her older years, just as she cared for our dear Asha.

Many special people have come into our lives over the years to help keep this dream going. Jim and Deirdre (DD) from Australia have always been there in the hard times, not only with financial support, but with spiritual support and good advice. Now they are about to set up an organization in Australia in order to help to raise funds (Hope Mobilization Australia). The organization Lamb Watcher from Brazil, formed by our friend Ulisses Sabara, has been a huge help. Also friends such as Pastor Welbr Santos, and Assembly of God under his leadership, helped me pay my rent when my bank card just wasn't up to the task. Pastor Joliam Sampaio bought clothes for all the kids for many years and paid for their school fees. He also brought candy, when he learned that the kids would chew gum they picked up on the streets. Sarah

EPILOGUE

Symons and Her Future Coalition sponsored kids for over 15 years and, along with DD and Jim, kept the school going when its other funding was withdrawn at one point.

Marco Romero and his church outside Boston, USA supported the work almost single handedly for over a year. Tony Rodrigues was instrumental, raising money in America, as were Ima, Mariluce, Daniel, Neto, Cleusa, Silvio Simoes, Antonio, Thallison, Betinho and many others. Some collected recycling cans to raise money for us in Nepal and some raised funds in other ways. Luigi Ricioppo helped release my burden around my own family's needs by helping me send David to Ireland for college. Dalila Barros, a director at MCM Brazil, was always raising money for us, coin by coin. And of course there's been Hope Force, Crossroads, Atlas Free, Bonhoeffer Cafe and many other generous organizations and friends.

Marcelo Bevilacqua came to Nepal in 2008 and Kelly Pinero came in 2009. They met here, got married and ended up staying for ten years. They only left because their son, who was born in Nepal, needed heart surgery and four years of medical follow up. Now they are in Romania, working to open a home for the trafficked children of that country. Igor Santos came in 2012 and met his wife Rute here in Nepal. They went back to Brazil and returned here married, and they are still here today. Rute, who has a degree in International Business, informally oversees the Beautiful Bride training center (where girls learn beautician skills) and has also taught many of our girls to bake.

Marsha and Bryon Skaggs came in 2017 and stayed seven years. They fostered and mentored some of our teenage boys who were in need of special attention and care. Marsha worked with Jane, Rose and our doctor, Gisele, to set up the NEST, a counseling and education support center. Dr. Gisele Sole came in 2017 and continues to serve selflessly and very effectively as a member of our team.

My Family

My wife Rose (her proper name is Rosmari) is a passionate person. She was born and raised on a farm, so she wasn't a city girl. But, since the day she met me in the Baptist Church in Mato Grosso, Brazil, her life has become very different. When we met, my life was very unstable. Rose became like an anchor from God. Going to Nepal for 20 plus years surely wasn't in her life plan! Our lives became much less predictable, but more adventurous.

We have traveled to many nations. Sometimes, when people invite us and sponsor the trip, we enjoy good hotels in beautiful places, and sometimes we stay at cheap hotels on our own. We have lived in big houses and small houses—and of course we'll never forget the budget hotel we called home when we first moved here. Rose has never complained. Even when we were in the Baptist College together and she had no new shoes for her piano recital, even when our refrigerator had almost nothing in it—she was always happy. That aspect of her character gave her the resilience to face very hard moments, such as when she almost died from an infection in 2008 or when I got sick with typhoid fever.

In 2022, Rose lost her mother suddenly, while she was visiting us in Nepal. That was the worst moment of her life. I've never seen her more distressed. After the funeral in Brazil, Rose spent some time in deep mourning, processing her pain. She actually considered not coming back to Nepal. But even through her suffering, Rose decided to fulfill her calling and return to Nepal.

EPILOGUE

The hard moments of this experience have left marks on Rose's soul for sure, but she never stopped "being a mother," as Dr. José challenged her to do back in 2000. I, personally, could never have gotten this far in my own life and calling without her. Her company, her work, her perspective, her encouragement and even her criticism always led me in good directions.

One night, on a trip to visit David (my son) while he was studying in the USA, we went for dinner and he asked me, "Dad, can I ask you a question? I won't promise to follow what you say, but I want to hear your opinion about it." Then he hit me with this question: "Should I graduate and make money in business, or should I follow the same calling that you have, to serve the hurting women and children of the world? Because sometimes I feel called to do that too."

The question made me dizzy, but without reflecting I hit him right back: "If you want to get to your fifties with a good retirement plan or assets, go to make money and donate to those who are doing the work. But, if you want to get to your fifties without savings, and without even a house, but having a great sense of accomplishment seeing many kids restored and living good lives, feeling something which money can't buy, then follow that calling."

I could see shock in David's eyes, but it seems he took the second advice, because soon after that he moved back to Nepal, and now he is working on staff for us at Apple.

David had a painful experience when he was 12 years old, when we were at a fancy restaurant with some sponsors in Brazil. He went to the bathroom and—despite the fact that he was clean and wearing good clothes—because David is black, the manager assumed he was a street kid looking for food and threw him out of the restaurant. When I noticed David was taking too long to come back from the bathroom, I went to look for him and saw the restaurant owner pushing him out the door. I explained that he was my son, and the owner realized his mistake and became very apologetic. I went back to that table unsure whether to protest by walking out, or if that would make David even more embarrassed. It was a very sad moment for David, a moment of pain and shame. But it seems that situations like that one — which David continued to face in Brazil and also in Nepal, the USA and Ireland, due to the color of his skin—inspired him to be a protector of others. I always tell the kids that we can let our pain be a wall that blocks us, or we can let it be a scar that hurts at times, but eventually heals and becomes a memorial which we carry to help others.

My daughter Asha seems to be the same way. She is involved in our work at every step, participating in events and seminars, listening to stories of survivors or people still in trouble, taking care of volunteers and donors and sharing about our work. I can see she is serving and involved because this is her calling too, not just the calling of her parents. Being Nepalese by birth adds more fuel to her fire, as she cannot bear to see her people in such trouble. Asha is getting ready to go to university, where she plans to study psychology and become a counselor. I constantly see her working passionately, listening, learning and improving herself so she can better serve others.

When we first came to Nepal, we thought we would stay for just a couple of years, set up an organization to fight human trafficking, and then head back to Brazil. Today, as I write these lines, we have been in Nepal for 24 years and counting.

EPILOGUE

It wasn't our original plan, but we thank God for it. We've gotten to have the most beautiful experience of having a family of people from many different nations. We love Nepal and its people. We have a big family here—hundreds of kids who call us father and mother, or uncle and aunt. But, regardless of what they call us, they are truly our sons and daughters.

What a sweet trap to come to Nepal planning to stay just two years and instead getting a family here and staying for our whole lives. Working from Nepal, helping to launch homes in Cambodia, Bangladesh and Thailand, welcoming and mentoring nonprofit leaders working in other countries, and raising young women and men who are serving in many countries, we have been able to reach more than 30 nations of the earth. The dream of that little boy delivering newspapers has come true.

Nepalese Home leadership team; December, 2019.

The Silva family today: David, Rose, Silvio and Asha.

Silvio and Rose; October, 2022.

If you're moved by these stories, we invite you to play a part in keeping this work going.

You can help provide more children in Nepal with dignity, hope and the chance to dream again.

To give in USD or BRL, visit:
www.aogenepal.org/PowerofDignity

To give in CAD, visit:
www.ally.org/PowerofDignity

Silvio Silva

Silvio Silva is the co-founder, with his wife Rose, of The Apple of God's Eyes in Nepal. They have walked alongside hundreds of girls on their journey to freedom, dignity and independence, including raising the first generation of girls who are now leaders in the organization. Silvio also helped to launch and support The Apple of God's Eyes projects in Cambodia, Thailand Bangladesh and most recently, Romania (in start-up phase). Silvio mentors and supports nonprofit leaders around the world. Prior to starting The Apple of God's Eyes, he served as a pastor of two congregations in Brazil. He and Rose are the parents of two young adults, David and Asha, and devoted Uncle and Aunty to hundreds of kids in Nepal, whose lives are now full of hope thanks to the loving, individualized and long term care they received at The Apple of God's Eyes.

Sarah Symons

Sarah Symons is the Founder and Executive Director of Her Future Coalition, an international charity combating human trafficking and other forms of gender-based violence with education and holistic support. Sarah and her organization have been proud partners and friends of Apple of God's Eyes for over 16 years.

Since 2005, Her Future Coalition has served more than 6,000 survivors and high risk girls in India, Nepal, Cambodia,Thailand and most recently, Kenya. Sarah is the author/co-author of four books, including *This is No Ordinary Joy* (available on Amazon) which shares the journey of her work with trafficking survivors, and *Standing in the Way*, co-authored with Anjali Tamang—who grew up at Apple and whose story is also featured in *The Power of Dignity*.

Printed in Great Britain
by Amazon